Kingdom Living Here and Now

A Life of Joy, Power, and Praise

Kingdom Living Here and Now

A Life of Joy, Power, and Praise

Malcolm Smith

Kingdom Living Here and Now: The Life of Joy, Power, and Praise by Malcolm Smith
ISBN 0-88270-692-6
Library of Congress Catalog Card Number: 96-84875
Copyright © 1996 by BRIDGE-LOGOS *Publishers*

Published by:
BRIDGE-LOGOS *Publishers*
North Brunswick Corporate Center
1300 Airport Road, Suite E
North Brunswick, NJ 08902

Table of Contents

Prologue

They had decided to leave in the early afternoon. There was nothing to stay for, but nothing to go home to either.

Now their feet dragged aimlessly on the road that wound its seven miles to Emmaus. Their conversation was spasmodic, rehashing the details over and over. It was only a few days since they had traveled eagerly into Jerusalem in the full expectancy that Jesus would declare Himself as Messiah. Their dreams of Israel's glory had evaporated in the stench of blood at Golgotha.

Absorbed in their grief, they did not notice the person drawing near, so His kindly voice startled them: "What are these words that you are exchanging with one another as you are walking?" (Luke 24:17).

They stopped and stared at the stranger. Neither of them recognized Him; but that was not strange, for tens of thousands of pilgrims were in the vicinity for Passover. The question amazed one of the disciples, who was named Cleopas. His whole world had collapsed into one pile of fragments labeled, "Jesus Messiah Dead." He supposed all Jerusalem was in mourning with him. He blurted out, "Are You the only one visiting Jerusalem and unaware of the things which have happened here in these days?" (Luke 24:18).

The stranger's brow wrinkled as He asked, "What things?" (Luke 24:19). Cleopas wanted to talk. This was the first person he had been able to speak to who was not drowned in sorrow along with him. The words poured out like a dam bursting. He hardly stopped for a breath.

"The things about Jesus the Nazarene, who was a prophet mighty in deed and word in the sight of God and all the people, and how the chief priests and our rulers delivered Him up to the sentence of death, and crucified Him. But we were hoping that it was He who was going to redeem Israel. Indeed, besides all this, it is the third day since these things happened. But also some women among us amazed us. When they were at the tomb early in the morning, and did not find His body, they came, saying that they had also seen a vision of angels, who said that He was alive. And some of those who were with us went to the tomb and found it just exactly as the women also had said; but Him they did not see" (Luke 24:19-24). He almost choked as he spoke the last words.

They began to walk quietly on toward Emmaus again—only the crunch of their sandals on the sandy road broke the silence. Then the stranger spoke again, gently: "O foolish men and slow of heart to believe in

2

all that the prophets have spoken! Was it not necessary for the Christ to suffer these things and to enter into His glory?" (Luke 24:25-26).

Somewhere deep within the two disciples a flicker of life sputtered. The Messiah *supposed to suffer?* Enter into glory, yes—but *suffer?* They looked at one another, puzzled by the words.

The stranger began to enlarge on His statement from the books of Moses. The ancient promise to the human race of a triumphant deliverer with a bruised heel and the promises to Abraham, Isaac, and Jacob. He asked their understanding of the blood of the sacrifices that flowed each day in the temple according to Levitical laws. He moved on to the prophets, quoting passages so familiar but bringing a light to them that made old words come alive. He explained that the Messiah was not only to have a glorious reign, but was also to be the suffering sacrificial lamb to take away the sin of His subjects.

Both of the disciples began to hope: *Maybe the women were right.* Maybe the Messiah had risen and been at the tomb that morning . . . maybe. Joy, a desire to live and tell the world what they were hearing, began to burn inside them. Suddenly they felt washed inside, alive—despair had gone.

A new world that had already dawned in the heavens now began to dawn within them: "But for you who fear My name the sun of righteousness will rise with healing in its wings; and you will go forth and skip about like calves from the stall" (Malachi 4:2).

They were at their gate all too soon. Long shadows were thrown across the street by the setting sun. Cleopas felt like he was about to view a glory he had never seen before. The stranger was bidding them farewell, but the two disciples would have none of it. They had to hear more, and they constrained Him to stay the night.

The three of them were reclining on the couches around the table, about to eat, when it occurred to Cleopas that he had not yet asked the stranger His name. Then the stranger reached out and took the bread off the table. The first reaction of Cleopas was shock. The stranger, in taking the bread, had assumed the position of host, the master of the house. The sense of shock passed in a moment as Cleopas realized he *wanted* this man to be master of his house.

The stranger took the bread, blessed it, then broke it and handed it to them. Whether it was the way He held the bread and blessed it, bringing back memories of the days of miracles in Galilee, Cleopas couldn't tell. All he knew was that suddenly they knew who this One was. *He was Jesus Messiah, the Lord of Glory.* It was as if they had always known, yet now they were seeing Him for the first time. The disciples' mouths fell open and they stared at each other and then at Jesus.

Then He was gone. The broken bread on the table was the only proof someone had been there. Cleopas leaped to his feet and almost shouted with a joy from another world: "Were not our hearts burning within us while He was speaking to us on the road, while He was explaining the Scriptures to us?" (Luke 24:32).

It was not the end, but the beginning. The long awaited kingdom was here and now—and they had just received their first lesson of how to live in its joy and praise.

1

Rebellion in Paradise

"You will be like God."
Genesis 3:5

It was the dawn of history. Like the fish, birds, insects, and animals before him, man was a creature issuing out of the creative word of the Creator. But unlike them, he was a finite copy of the Creator. He was made lord of the planet, subject to no other creature on it. He was a *person* made in the image of the original person, the Creator, and so able to fellowship and commune with Him, person with person. All other creatures obeyed the Creator instinctively, as He had programmed them to do. This one and his companion, however, were to choose freely to love God, trust and obey Him, and fellowship with Him. Their work on the planet was to subdue it and, side by side with all future persons, glorify God and bring about His wise love purposes.

Then into this innocent beauty came Satan—the distorted one, lord of darkness—and with lying words,

7

called the woman to make a choice about God. The couple had seen His commands as love communicating infinite wisdom, desiring their highest good and providing full, abundant life at all levels of consciousness.

The serpent gave her an alternative view of God. He was saying that God's commands were not born of love, but rather to keep the couple in ignorance and from a life that truly fulfilled all their potential. She need no longer be a dependent mortal, God would no longer be necessary, for she would be like God herself.

If man, made in God's image, had the power of free, unprogrammed choice, he was not truly man until he had chosen. He could rule the earth only if he made the conscious choice to be the creature trusting and obeying God's wise love commands. So a choice must be made: God's will or self-will.

"You will be like God," the serpent told the woman, and the lie stirred desires and feelings inside her that she had never known before. Being like God, her world would center around her and she would enjoy the luxury of having every creature do her bidding and pleasing her. She would be free from all authority, all restraints, allowed to live to herself in godlike independence.

Eve believed the lie and spoke to her husband to bring him with her into the suicidal rebellion against the Most High. Adam joined her in the act of disobedience with his eyes wide open, knowing the insanity of what they were doing. He added to his rebellion the idolatry of loving and trusting his wife more than the truth he had heard from the Creator who gave her to him.

The couple were now joined to the lie. The image of God in them that was expressed in their natural powers was blitzed and twisted by it. Their powers of reason were off center. Where once all their reasoning began from the starting point of God's revelation, it now began from the assumption that their own deductions were more trustworthy.

Under the control of darkness, new emotions replaced the love, joy, and peace of life under God. New dark emotions of anger, rage, bitterness, hatred, and envy came into being and were transmitted to all who were born of the man and woman. As humanity multiplied and moved out into the earth, it left behind a wake of pain and distress wherever it went. Because all now lived in the fantasy that they each were God and should be pleased and obeyed, they constantly fought each other to get their own way. The man and woman had taken the planet entrusted to them and, along with themselves, had joined it—and all their descendants—to the serpent.

The human race wrapped inside this couple would continue to spiral downward in its chosen slavery to the pseudo-god of darkness. In Romans 1:21-23, 25, 28-32, the history of the race is outlined:

> For even though they knew God, they did not honor Him as God, or give thanks; but they became futile in their speculations, and their foolish heart was darkened.
>
> Professing to be wise, they became fools, and exchanged the glory of the incorruptible God for an image in the form of corruptible man and of birds and four-footed animals and crawling creatures. . . .
>
> For they exchanged the truth of God for a lie, and worshiped and served the creature rather than the Creator. . . .

9

And just as they did not see fit to acknowledge God any longer, God gave them over to a depraved mind, to do those things which are not proper,

being filled with all unrighteousness, wickedness, greed, malice; full of envy, murder, strife, deceit, malice; they are gossips,

slanderers, haters of God, insolent, arrogant, boastful, inventors of evil, disobedient to parents,

without understanding, untrustworthy, unloving, unmerciful;

and, although they know the ordinance of God, that those who practice such things are worthy of death, they not only do the same, but also give hearty approval to those who practice them.

After they had sinned, the couple stumbled through the underbrush of Eden with a new sensation sending tremors through them. They were now experiencing emotions of shame and fear—and their basic fear was toward God. Their lover and friend was now the great enemy. It was His throne that they had tried to steal in their rebellion, and now the presence that had delighted them only accented their guilt and made them want to flee. God's presence reminded them that their rebellion was a fantasy, for no created creature could be God. While God was a reality in his mind, man could never live easily in the lie that he was God. He felt more at home with the darkness and the lie, aligned to Satan against God.

But God was not deterred by the distorted view man now had of Him, nor could His presence be escaped by

10

hiding in a few bushes. He loved the man He had created in His own image. Even in the newly acquired rebellious condition, one human was worth more to Him than His entire universe. From before time began, God had seen the rebellion and committed Himself to bringing man back to fellowship with Himself, achieving in man the grand purpose for which he had been created. Man would yet freely worship God and be the king of creation as had been originally appointed.

This act of rebellion inevitably brought about a natural retribution. God is life in Himself. All life, whether plant, animal, or human, whether physical, psychic, or spiritual, is from Him and is dependent on Him. To oppose Him is therefore to bring about separation from life, which is death. As soon as man entered into the rebellion against God, he died—having separated himself from the source of all life. Death is not ceasing to exist, but a state of being in which a spirit is cut off from life. Man now merely existed, groping after a meaning to life, rather than enjoying the fullness of life for which he had been made.

But there was more than a natural retribution in the results of the act of rebellion. God is the holy One. He who is positive righteousness must of necessity be active in His opposition to sin. In God, anger is not a passing emotion that boils or cools according to outward pressures—it is the unchanging set of His being in opposition to all that is not according to His holiness, which is the life and health of His creation.

If humanity were ever to have a reversal of the hideous results of sin and be restored to fellowship with God, his sin would have to be perfectly judged and wiped out. Humanity could not be welcomed back into fellowship with the holy One on any terms but absolute justice. Likewise, if the planet were to be won back from the dark lord who now had possession of it, it would have to be done in harmony with His justice.

But where in all the earth and in all time would there be a man who would be able to wrest the earth from Satan and render such an act of obedience to God as to atone for the guilt of the race? All men were under the authority of the darkness and the lie. Where could man run to from the just anger of God against his sin? Where could he find deliverance from his new master, the liar and destroyer?

He must flee from God by fleeing to Him.

What man must accomplish if he is ever to be right with God is of such a nature that only God could accomplish it.

The man, the woman, and the snake stood in the presence of the God against whom they were in rebellion. His judgment is pronounced upon their sin, but in His judgment is His salvation.

Addressing the serpent God said, "I will put enmity Between you and the woman, And between your seed and her seed; He shall bruise you on the head, And you shall bruise him on the heel" (Genesis 3:15).

There would be a conqueror, one sent by God, who would be a member of the race born of a woman as all other men. This one would deliver a crushing blow to the serpent and cause a total reversal of the situation the man and woman had brought humanity into.

It was *man* who had rebelled and who stood truly guilty before God. It was *man* who had handed over the kingdom entrusted to him to the serpent, and the promise stated that a man *of the race* would trample the dark lord under foot, crushing his rule over man. Such a triumph would cost the man who would be sent a wound on his heel, but that wounded foot would be a triumphant foot laid on the serpent's head.

The words that came to man were first of all a statement of *God's* intent and purpose; only in a secondary sense was it a promise to man. It therefore demanded nothing of man for its achievement. Any salvation that was of any use to man would have to be this way, for this was nothing man could do to achieve his own salvation. In this surrendering of himself to God's saving action in the coming one, he would be joined to the victory and would be in Satan's world but not of it.

These words were the fountainhead of all prophecy. From that time on, all religions of the world were divided into a simple two. There is the religion that comprises all the ways that call man to *be doing* something on his part in order that he may earn his acceptance with God. And there is the religion that began that day in Eden, born of God's own revelation of Himself, that announces God *has done* all for man by His sent One—who does for man what he could never do for himself.

Out of all the millions of words that Eve must have spoken after their rebellion, only one phrase came down to us over the centuries. The fact that this particular one is recorded suggests it is of great importance. It was at the birth of Cain that the immortal sentence was spoken: "I have gotten a manchild with the help of the Lord" (Genesis 4:1). The expression is better translated perhaps in the margin of the New American Standard Version: "I have gotten a man, the Lord."

She had heard the promise from the Lord and clearly understood that the deliverer would be a real man, born of a woman. She had further understood that *this man would be none other than the Lord Himself.* The couple

13

understood that the only man who could deliver the race would have to be God as well as man.

As she looked at her child, the first human to be born of a woman, she wrongly supposed him to be the promised deliverer. Her statement, though wrong in its timing, gives us the understanding our earliest ancestors had concerning the coming One.

Centuries after the rebellion had begun, a baby was born. At the naming ceremony the father showed his hope in the deliverer and what He would do: "Now he called his name Noah, saying, 'This one shall give us rest from our work and from the toil of our hands arising from the ground which the Lord has cursed'" (Genesis 5:29).

The name *Noah* means to settle, rest, remain. Throughout the Scriptures this same word is translated to mean enjoying rest by being freed from irksome toil and unpleasant conditions. Lamech thought his son was the deliverer, and so called him the rest bringer, the curse remover. He was wrong, of course, for Noah was not the sent One; but we are told that those communities of faith expected the crushing of the serpent's head to usher in a rest and holy joy because the curse would be removed. It follows that the person who would remove the curse that God had laid would Himself have to be God.

Instead of being the remover of the curse, Noah was the one to bring the human race through the flood of God's judgment and step out into the virgin earth to be the father of the next episode in the history of the race. Noah passed on the promise and hope of the deliverer to his children, who had already started to corrupt themselves as their forefathers had before them.

14

2

From Idolater to Patriarch

The nations that sprang from Noah and his sons were not different from man before the Flood of judgment. They moved further from the truth into the lie, spiraling downward into the darkness. But the lie could not be enjoyed while there was even an intellectual understanding of God, let alone the awareness of His presence. Each time they were faced with the concept of the only true and utterly holy God, they were faced with their true guilt and the impossibility of the lie in which they lived.

To avoid facing their guilt they simply removed God from their minds, replacing Him with a multitude of gods and goddesses who were the extension of their impurity, cruelty, and lust for power.

> For even though they knew God, they did
> not honor Him as God, or give thanks; but

15

they became futile in their speculations, and
their foolish heart was darkened.

Professing to be wise, they became fools,
and exchanged the glory of the incorruptible
God for an image in the form of corruptible
man and of birds and four-footed animals
and crawling creatures.

Romans 1:21-23

One such center of idolatry was Ur in Chaldea.
It was here that some of the descendants of Shem,
son of Noah, had come to settle. One of them was
Abram, son of Terah. The city had long ago
distorted the knowledge of the true God given them
by Noah into the worship of a moon deity.

To Abram, the idolater of Ur, God made Himself
known: "The God of glory appeared to our father
Abraham when he was in Mesopotamia, before he
lived in Haran" (Acts 7:2).

The details of the revelation we do not know,
but the most important thing is *what* God did, not
how He did it. Abram did not deserve a revelation
of the person of God, having done nothing to earn
or merit the voice of God that spoke to him in the
pagan darkness. He, too, was part of the rebellion.
*The revelation came because God was love, mercy, and
grace, not because of who Abram was.*

He called Abram to separate himself from the
idolatry of Ur and journey to a land that would be
shown to him as he went:

Go forth from your country,
And from your relative
And from your father's house,

16

> To the land which I will show you;
> And I will make you a great nation,
> And I will bless you,
> And make your name great;
> And so you shall be a blessing;
> And I will bless those who bless you,
> And the one who curses you I will curse.
> And in you all the families of the earth
> shall be blessed.
>
> Genesis 12:1-3

Abram obeyed and went, following the voice that led them along the caravan routes that took them westward, across the River Euphrates and into Canaan.

In the years that Abram lived in the land in tents, the Lord reiterated His promise to him, and expanded and explained it. Abram was to become the father of a vast multitude: "And I will make your descendants as the dust of the earth; so that if anyone can number the dust of the earth, then your descendants can also be numbered" (Genesis 13:16).

On another occasion God took him outside and said, "Now look toward the heavens, and count the stars, if you are able to count them." And He said to him, "So shall your descendants be" (Genesis 15:5).

The focal point of the promise lay far in the future. Abram was to have a descendant through whom all nations of the earth would be blessed: "And I will bless those who bless you, And the one who curses you I will curse. And in you all the families of the earth shall be blessed" (Genesis 12:3).

17

The deliverer, who would be a son of the human race descending through Noah, was now specifically pointed out as being a descendant of Abram. The multitude of descendants and the land in which they lived was but the necessary womb for the coming deliverer who was the ultimate focus of the promise.

If a nation of multitudes was to claim Abram as its father, he had to have a least one son to start such a nation on its way. But Abram and Sarai had no son, and their advanced age made it ridiculous to cherish such a hope any longer.

So Abram was faced with God's word that stated he would have a son who would be the gateway to all the other promises; and the evidence in his wife's body that such a word was foolish, impossible and, in fact, a lie. The promise God made forced Abram to make a choice about the character of God: Was He a liar by the evidence that faced Abram in the natural world, or would God provide a deliverer even though common sense said that the very idea was nonsense?

It was the same choice that Eve wrestled with at the original temptation, and that every man at some time is called to make: *Is God utterly trustworthy, or is He to be rejected in favor of man's intellect and common sense?*

Abram made the choice. He abandoned himself to what God said, and in so doing disassociated himself from the world built on the lie that rested in favor of man's common sense. When he did, he was accepted by God and all his guilt and involvement in the lie was covered over as if it never had been. This was not because of anything Abram had done, but because he accepted what God was to do. Not on the basis of merit or desert, but on the basis of God's ability to keep His word. This is what the Scriptures mean by *faith*, and in his faith Abram became a message in flesh as to the true nature of the faith that links us to God. God changed his name to Abraham, meaning "father of a multitude," so that he carried in his name his confession of faith.

According to the word of God, the promised son was born to Abraham and Sarah in their old age. Through the son of promise, Isaac, the final Son of promise would come, and through Him the world would be blessed.

There was no further addition to the unfolding prophecies of the coming man of promise until the son of Isaac, Jacob, whose name had been changed to Israel, gathered his sons to his deathbed. One of these rugged sons that stood around his bed would become the bearer of the promise. When Judah, whose name means "praise", knelt beside his father's bed and Jacob's hands were laid on him, the matter of the promised One was raised:

> Judah, your brothers shall praise you;
> Your hand shall be on the neck of your enemies;
> Your father's sons shall bow down to you.
> Judah is a lion's whelp;
> From the prey, my son, you have gone up.
> He couches, he lies down as a lion,
> And as a lion, who dares rouse him up?
> The scepter shall not depart from Judah,

> Nor the ruler's staff from between his feet,
> Until Shiloh comes,
> And to him shall be the obedience of the peoples.
>
> Genesis 49:8-10

From Israel's family are to come twelve tribes that will comprise the nation of Israel, the great nation promised to Abraham. Judah was now singled out from his brothers as the tribe that would hold the scepter, the ruler's staff, until Shiloh—the Lord—would come.

But that office was a borrowed kingship. The royal family of Judah would be a shadow anticipating One called Shiloh. *Shiloh* means, "He whose right it is." A king from Judah's family would reign over the nation, but only until He whose right it was to reign should come. When He came, Judah's royal family would yield the crown to Him and He would wear it forever. Only that One had the right to rule over God's people.

This Lion of the tribe of Judah was the conqueror, the One who would remove the curse and bring the blessing of Abraham to the world. He would be the desire of mankind. To Him they would flee from the darkness to the light, for said Israel, "To him shall be the obedience of the peoples." God would not only place an enmity in the heart of His people against Satan, but also a love for His king—they would delight to bow to Him.

For many centuries it did not look as if there would be a promised nation, let alone a king to reign over them. They were kept as slaves by Egypt for hundreds of years, delivered by Moses, and then held a precarious possession of Canaan under a series of judges. But finally the fulfillment of God's Word began to be seen. After Israel's abortive attempt to have a king in order to be on a par with other nations, God's chosen king of the tribe of Judah was anointed. The first Lion of Judah to hold the scepter until *Shiloh* came was David, son of Jesse, a shepherd boy who came from Bethlehem in the tract of land belonging to the tribe of Judah.

During David's reign, Israel became a powerful nation under God, enjoying all the borders and multitude of people that had been promised:

> So the Lord gave Israel all the land which He had sworn to give to their fathers, and they possessed it and lived in it.
>
> And the Lord gave them rest on every side, according to all that He had sworn to their fathers, and no one of all their enemies stood before them; the Lord gave all their enemies into their hand.
>
> Not one of the good promises which the Lord had made to the house of Israel failed; all came to pass.
>
> Joshua 21:43-45

After David was established as king there was a further statement made concerning the promised king and the coming kingdom:

> When your days are complete and you lie down with your fathers, I will raise up your descendant after you, who will come forth from you, and I will establish his kingdom.

> He shall build a house for My name, and
> I will establish the throne of his kingdom
> forever. . . .
> And your house and your kingdom shall
> endure before Me forever; your throne shall
> be established forever.
>
> 2 Samuel 7:12-13, 16

Only in the most elementary sense did this speak of Solomon, the son of David who was to reign after him. Ultimately, it could only speak of the final King, the blesser of the world that would spring from the line of David's descendants. In his psalms, David sang of the sureness of God's promise to him, and through him to the whole world.

> My covenant I will not violate,
> Nor will I alter the utterance of My lips.
> Once I have sworn by My holiness;
> I will not lie to David.
> His . . . [seed] shall endure forever,
> And his throne as the sun before Me.
> It shall be established forever like the
> moon,
> And the witness in the sky is faithful.
>
> Psalms 89:34-37

David realized that although he reigned over Israel, *Shiloh* would rule the world. He sang of the coronation of the Lord's Anointed One when He was established as Lord of the earth. David saw that all nations would be threatened, raging in fury, for in His coronation they would be faced with *their* king, and could no longer live in the fantasy of absolute power independent of God. Rage as they may,

God's promise would be fulfilled and the Lion of the tribe of Judah would conquer. His song is recorded in Psalms 2:1-9 and 110:1-2:

> Why are the nations in an uproar,
> And the peoples devising a vain thing?
> The kings of the earth take their stand,
> And the rulers take counsel together
> Against the Lord and against His Anointed:
> "Let us tear their fetters apart,
> And cast away their cords from us!"
>
> He who sits in the heavens laughs,
> The Lord scoffs at them.
> Then He will speak to them in His anger
> And terrify them in His fury:
> "But as for Me, I have installed My King
> Upon Zion, My holy mountain."
>
> "I will surely tell of the decree of the Lord:
> He said to Me, 'Thou art My Son,
> Today I have begotten Thee.
> Ask of Me, and I will surely give the nations as Thine inheritance,
> And the very ends of the earth as Thy possession.
> Thou shalt break them with a rod of iron,
> Thou shalt shatter them like earthenware.'"

23

> The Lord says to my Lord:
> "Sit at My right hand,
> Until I make Thine enemies a foot-
> stool for Thy feet."
> The Lord will stretch forth Thy
> strong scepter from Zion, saying,
> "Rule in the midst of Thine
> enemies."

After David's death those who had the faith of Abraham looked eagerly for the Anointed One—or Messiah, as it is in Hebrew. Prophets began to arise telling of who He was. Of all the prophets, Isaiah frequented more courtrooms of David's descendants and spoke more of the coming One than any other. On one occurrence the Spirit came upon him and he addressed the whole house of David, his contemporaries, and those yet unborn:

> Listen now, O house of David! Is it too
> slight a thing for you to try the patience of
> men, that you will try the patience of my God
> as well?
> Therefore the Lord Himself will give you
> a sign: Behold, a virgin will be with child
> and bear a son, and she will call His name
> Immanuel.
>
> Isaiah 7:13-14

The child would be born of a human mother. He would share the common humanity of the race but be unlike any other person of the race, for His mother would be a *virgin*. He would be Immanuel: God with us (Matthew 1:23). In a mystery of mysteries, the eternal

God would be born a man. *The God who had promised to save the rebel man was going to enter the race to be that Savior.*

The prophecy held Isaiah and thrilled him. He described the coming One in chapter 9, verses 6 and 7:

> For a child will be born to us, a son will
> be given to us;
> And the government will rest on His
> shoulders;
> And His name will be called Wonderful
> Counselor, Mighty God,
> Eternal Father, Prince of Peace.
> There will be no end to the increase of
> His government or of peace,
> On the throne of David and over his
> kingdom,
> To establish it and to uphold it with
> justice and righteousness
> From then on and forevermore.
> The zeal of the Lord of hosts will
> accomplish this.

He would be thoroughly human, a child born—and at the same time, a Son given as the gift to the race. He would be the Prince of Peace, achieving peace between man and God and man and man, as well as within man's own disturbed heart.

Isaiah spoke in the court of the king, but Micah addressed the villages, speaking of the same coming ruler of the people:

> But as for you, Bethlehem Ephrathah,
> Too little to be among the clans of
> Judah,

> From you One will go forth for Me to be
> ruler in Israel.
> His goings forth are from long ago,
> From the days of eternity.
>
> And He will arise and shepherd His
> flock
> In the strength of the Lord,
> In the majesty of the name of the Lord
> His God.
> And they will remain,
> Because at that time He will be great
> To the ends of the earth.
> And this One will be our peace.
>
> Micah 5:2, 4-5

Such a phrase describing this One could be understood only in terms of a man who was God. God He was from eternity, yet He would begin a temporal journey in Bethlehem. The unbeginning would begin, the Creator would live out the genuine history of a creature because He loved man and determined to save him from his guilt and his slavery to the lord of darkness.

Isaiah caught the vastness of what he was saying—the Lord Himself would visit this pocket of rebellion in His universe. But before He did so, a herald would come preparing His way:

> A voice is calling,
> "Clear the way for the Lord in the
> wilderness;
> Make smooth in the desert a highway for
> our God.
> Let every valley be lifted up,

And every mountain and hill be made
low;
And let the rough ground become a
plain,
And the rugged terrain a broad valley;
Then the glory of the Lord will be
revealed,
And all flesh will see it together;
For the mouth of the Lord has spoken."

Get yourself up on a high mountain,
O Zion, bearer of good news,
Lift up your voice mightily,
O Jerusalem, bearer of good news;
Lift it up, do not fear.
Say to the cities of Judah,
"Here is your God!"
Behold, the Lord God will come with
might,
With His arm ruling for Him.

Behold, His reward is with Him,
And His recompense before Him.
Like a shepherd He will tend His flock,
In His arm He will gather the lambs,
And carry them in His bosom;
He will gently lead the nursing ewes.
Isaiah 40:3-5, 9-11

All the darkness would flee before the arrival of the
Lion of Judah. When Satan's head was smashed and the
blessing long promised to Abraham came, a new day
would dawn among men. Malachi, one of the last
prophets of Old Testament order, described this: "But
for you who fear My name the sun of righteousness will
rise with healing in its wings" (Malachi 4:2).

3

An End to Sacrifices

The coming deliverer was going to bring about a complete rebirth in the rebelling heart of man: hatred for Satan would be implanted in man's heart, and friendship with God would be reestablished. *There could be no friendship reestablished, no fellowship enjoyed unless the sin of man was justly dealt with.* That was the way it had to be—it is the law of God's being, for He is the holy One.

Holy is not an attribute of God; it is the way He is, His very essence.

When the Bible calls something holy, it means that the designated object or person is separated to God, or for God. When we say that the essence of God is holy, we are saying that He is separated to Himself, wholly for Himself. It further means that all creation looks only to Him and worships only Him. He is the eternal infinite noun, and all creation the adjective.

If this is the egoism of God, it is the only right egoism in the universe. He is the source of all, the only person from whom and in whom all persons receive their selfhood. He is the source of life, its only reason and its object. He is the ground of all law, natural and moral, the absolute from which all rational creatures derive the concept of right and wrong. Law and justice are not abstract concepts outside of God, but are expressions of Him, the holy One.

The creature's first and final duty, and only true life, is to take his place as a creature and acknowledge God as the all in all of life. When man grasped to himself that place, the lie of pride had begun on the planet.

Man's sin is not merely negative thinking or a foolish alternative lifestyle. It is rebellion against the holy One and therefore a rebellion against life Himself, a plunging into the world of the living dead. Wedded thus to sin, man became the object of the holy wrath of God.

Sin is the defiance of God's holiness. It is the creature setting his will against the only Will, proclaiming himself independent, the beginning of another law. *For God to deny His moral law would be to deny Himself.* If He let sin go unpunished and His justice be mocked, we would have the absurdity of a God who was less than Himself. He *must* move out against sin and judge it with His holy wrath. His anger is not a passing mood, but the eternal necessity of His unchanging self.

But God is love, and He wills that the rebel man come back into His fellowship. This love is the message of the Bible, but we have never heard that message until we understand that it is *holy love*—a love that cannot overlook the necessity of His justice punishing all that rises against Him. For God to love man without fulfilling the demand of justice would be to deny Himself, which would be to cease being God.

God's love is not a sentimental affection, but an eternal love founded on His holiness. *God, by the necessity of who He is, cannot bring man back into fellowship with Himself without fully satisfying His justice that demands punishment of sin.*

But if man was exposed to God's wrath, he would be eternally destroyed from God's presence. In the holy love of God we are faced with the God who Himself bears the full demand of justice on behalf of man. Man would be forgiven and welcomed into fellowship, but only because God has rendered the satisfaction to Himself that His justice requires. His love cannot contradict His justice—it is holy love.

The end result is not only forgiveness for man but the shining forth of the holiness of God. The sin of man has revealed a holiness that is not vindictive but rather *loves* the rebel, and at the same time vindicates God. In loving man He has not swept His law and justice under the rug, but exalted and glorified them to infinity.

Faith is man's rest in God's holiness. It begins with the sinner agreeing with His justice, admitting himself the rebel. It finds its climax in the abandonment of the sinner to holy love, resting in God's faithfulness to Himself. Such faith knows of no struggle to please God, for it rests wholly on who God is and what He has provided.

The deliverer was to bring man a new heart, restore fellowship, and bring into existence a people saved from among the living dead. Until then the sinner was given a substitute that could bear his guilt and assume his punishment. Through substitute animals man could know fellowship with God until the deliverer established reconciliation forever.

Man could not initiate his salvation. The substitutionary sacrifices were God's gift to man, foreshadowing the day when the penalty of man's sin would be fully borne by God.

From the first promise of the deliverer, man was given the ritual of sacrifice—a place and method to come and claim God as his salvation. The first recorded coming and receiving of salvation was that of the son of Adam, called Abel. Throughout the history of Israel whenever man responded to God's justice and love in faith, animal sacrifice was present.

It was among the Israelites at Sinai that the system of sacrifice in the hands of a priesthood was formally used. On Mount Sinai, Moses was shown the splendor and glory of heaven, and God gave him a pattern from which to build on earth a tent that would be a symbolic visual aid of heaven itself and the heavenly realm. It was called the tabernacle, or the tent of meeting.

The simple structure began with an outer court fenced by curtains. Within the court was the tabernacle proper, a tent that housed two rooms. The first room was the holy place; the second, separated by a thick veil, was the holy of holies. In this second room God's presence was manifest in a blazing light over a box called the ark of the covenant. Here was the center of Israel, their God, their king among them.

God provided for the sin of the nation of Israel by giving them a priesthood, which was headed by a high priest who was given by God to be the representative man for the whole nation. He carried the nation in himself, and in him they communed with God.

The priesthood officiated at the God-given offerings. For every spiritual need and mood of the people there was provided offerings wherein God took it upon Himself to bring the people to Himself. In all the offerings blood had to be shed. Even the unbloody cereal offering had to be accompanied by one of the blood offerings. The people must never forget that if sin were to be forgiven, it must be paid for by the sacrifice of a life.

The very center of the whole sacrificial system was on that one day in which God proclaimed all that He was doing. It was called the day of atonement. On this day the offering included all other offerings of the year and, in a final sense, summed them up so much that through this offering the high priest, as the representative of the covenant people, could go into the immediate presence and commune with God behind the veil. In his being there, every covenant Israelite saw himself there, carried in his representative.

But in all of this, sin was not *dealt* with, only covered over. The blood on the mercy seat each year was a promise of something better, a finale when sin would be put away. It was the shadow of a coming substance. The root of a flower awaiting the day of blooming.

Every sacrifice and high priest awaited the coming of the deliverer who would vindicate God's holiness and bring man into His kingdom.

The prophets spoke of a day when all sacrifices would be unnecessary. The substance of which the shadow spoke would have come, sin would be wiped out, and the long-promised change of heart come to pass:

> "But this is the covenant which I will make with the house of Israel after those days," declares the Lord, "I will put My law within them, and on their heart I will write it; and I will be their God, and they shall be My people."
>
> Jeremiah 31:33

Another prophet, Daniel, received a revelation from God regarding the coming deliverer, or Messiah, God's Anointed One:

> "Seventy weeks have been decreed for your people and your holy city, to finish the transgression, to make an end of sin, to make atonement for iniquity, to bring in everlasting righteousness, to seat up vision and prophecy, and to anoint the most holy place."
>
> Daniel 9:24

The term *weeks* is not to be understood as weeks of days. Prophets sometimes spoke in terms of a day being equal to a year. Thus Daniel's prophecy

34

meant seventy weeks of years or 490 years. *Within the next five centuries the purposes of God through His Anointed One would be accomplished.* This period of time, said the messenger, was *"decreed."*

When the new covenant would be effective, the old covenant with its Levitical offerings and sacrifices would come to an end. There would be no more use for them. Every blood sacrifice in the temple existed because sin had not yet been put away. With the new covenant, with its proclamation that sin and iniquity were remembered no more—or as Daniel now put it, transgression was finished—sin had come to an end, and everlasting righteousness would be brought in. So there would be no more need for temple sacrifices.

The messengers said that this ending of sacrifice and offering would take place in the middle of the last week. If we take a day as being a year, he is saying that *a little more than three years after the making known of the Messiah the Levitical sacrifices would be brought to a close.*

What a message! There would be a return to the land, and after an exact period of time, Messiah will come. Though nations rage, rise, and fall, God's purpose goes on. Messiah's coming would be marked by His being cut off and left alone in His achieving of the sixfold purpose of God's ancient covenant with man. This would mean the ending of the whole system that was summed up in the sacrifices and offerings for sin. A new day would dawn in Messiah's coming.

But the message didn't bring only hope; it brought horror, too. Although the message was their hope of a return to rebuild Jerusalem and await the Messiah, it went on to speak of the destruction of that city. A prince would come and destroy Jerusalem and the sanctuary—there would be a flood of war, desolation, and horror.

The horizon was radiant with the Messiah's accomplishment and black with the horror of the total destruction of the earthly center of the old covenant and the Levitical system. The Hebrew word *decreed* is descriptive of a tailor cutting off enough cloth to complete a garment. God was cutting off the next five centuries to fully complete His purpose, which He listed in six specific goals:

> To finish the transgression
> To make an end of sin
> To make atonement for iniquity
> To bring in everlasting righteousness
> To seal up vision and prophecy
> To anoint the most holy place

This sixfold purpose was a more detailed explanation of what Jeremiah had spoken of as the new covenant.

After sixty-nine of the seventy "weeks" had passed, Messiah would come. The remaining "week" was descriptive of Messiah's work and the accomplishing of the sixfold purpose.

The coming of the long-awaited Messiah would be marked by His "cutting off" and "having nothing" or no one. A lonely, cut-off Messiah! Not the conquering king the Israelites were looking for?

The last week is again described as the making of "a firm covenant with the many for one week." In the Hebrew, the covenant spoken of is not one that would be made that week—but one that was previously made and is now *becoming effective,* or *now bringing its conditions into force.*

What covenant is this that in the last years of this decreed period would become effective? We know the sixfold goal of the period and have noted the marked parallel to the new covenant. The new covenant was but a further statement of God's promise, or covenant, to send a deliverer and accomplish salvation. In the cutting off of Messiah that ancient covenant would come into force and become effective.

If the coming One was to achieve all that the offerings spoke of, it is no surprise to find the description of His work in language associated with the sacrificial system. Isaiah was the prophet whose ministry began with a vision of the holiness of God. He saw very clearly that if sin was to be put away by the deliverer, the deliverer must bear the cost.

Isaiah gives a prophetic picture of the king who should come and reign over His universal kingdom, but he also describes the king as the suffering servant of the Lord. A suffering deliverer? Tragedy and triumph? Suffering and glory? How could the two come together? The prophet asked the question: "Who has believed our message? And to whom has the arm of the Lord been revealed?" (Isaiah 53:1).

Who would ever believe what he had to say? The Israelites must be prepared for a shock. Although He would reign over all nations, the first sight of Him would not be of a glorious king. The root out of David would be a wounded, suffering deliverer:

> For He grew up before Him like a tender shoot,
> And like a root out of parched ground;
> He has no stately form or majesty

> That we should look upon Him....
> He was despised and forsaken of men,
> A man of sorrows, and acquainted with
> grief;
> And like one from whom men hide their
> face,
> He was despised, and we did not esteem
> Him.
>
> Isaiah 53:2-3

He went on to describe the reason for such a situation:

> Surely our griefs He Himself bore,
> And our sorrows He carried;
> Yet we ourselves esteemed Him stricken,
> Smitten of God, and afflicted.
> But He was pierced through for our
> transgressions,
> He was crushed for our iniquities;
> The chastening for our well-being fell
> upon Him,
> And by His scourging we are healed.
>
> Isaiah 53:4-5

The word *bore* was a familiar word to the Hebrews. It was connected to the offerings for sin in the tabernacle and temple, especially with the day of atonement. In the making of an animal sacrifice for sin, the hands of the priest were laid on it, and the sins of the people confessed. The sin of the people was said to have been *borne* away by the sacrifice. In the same way, the coming One was to be the sacrifice for man—but He would not simply cover sin, He would bear it away.

38

In describing what He would do, Isaiah stated, "All of us like sheep have gone astray, Each of us has turned to his own way; But the Lord has caused the iniquity of us all To fall on Him" (Isaiah 53:6).

It was this One who was to come who gave meaning and sense to every animal that was sacrificed at the hand of the priest. He was the substance, and the sacrificial animals the shadow. Without the substance the shadow had no meaning.

The animals were insufficient and could never adequately bear away sin. Man had sinned with the full exercise of his choice, and a nonrational animal with no choice could never finally take man's place. But this One that the animals foreshadowed would choose to be the sacrifice—a *person* led to the altar.

> He was oppressed and He was afflicted,
> Yet He did not open His mouth; Like a lamb
> that is led to slaughter, And like a sheep that
> is silent before its shearers, So He did not
> open His mouth.
>
> Isaiah 53:7

Isaiah went on to speak of His death. This was an insolvable problem. How could the One who would rule forever come to death? But the prophet added insult to enigma. The matter of burial was of great importance to the ancients. The details of death were his memorial to posterity. The burial of Messiah was described: "His grave was assigned to be with wicked men, Yet with a rich man in His death; Although He had done no violence, Nor was there any deceit in His mouth" (Isaiah 53:9). A sinless Messiah whose burial would be with the wicked as well as the rich.

But there was more beyond. The days of the dead Messiah would be prolonged. He who was the final sin offering would see that what He had done was accomplished: "But the Lord was pleased To crush Him, putting Him to grief; If He would render Himself as a guilt offering, He will see His offspring, He will prolong His days, And the good pleasure of the Lord will prosper in His hand" (Isaiah 53:10).

Because of the Messiah's being the final offering, He would put away sin, and all that Jeremiah and Daniel had spoken of would come to pass.

David, who foreshadowed Shiloh, felt not only His glory as universal ruler, but also felt His suffering. In Psalm 22, he describes a suffering that he went through, but in his description goes far beyond what had happened to him. His psalm became an echo of a future suffering that the final king would endure:

> My God, my God, why hast Thou forsaken me?
> Far from my deliverance are the words of my groaning.
>
> But I am a worm, and not a man
> A reproach of men, and despised by the people.
> All who see me sneer at me;
> They separate with the lip, they wag the head, saying,
> "Commit yourself to the Lord; let Him deliver him;
> Let Him rescue him, because He delights in him."

I am poured out like water,
And all my bones are out of joint;
My heart is like wax;
It is melted within me.
My strength is dried up like a potsherd,
And my tongue cleaves to my jaws;
And Thou dost lay me in the dust of
death.

For dogs have surrounded me;
A band of evildoers has encompassed
me;
They pierced my hands and my feet.
I can count all my bones.
They look, they stare at me;
They divide my garments among them,
And for my clothing they cast lots
                            Psalms 22:1, 6-8, 14-18

But again there was a glory beyond, for the One who
so suffered would praise God in the middle of the people
of God: "I will tell of Thy name to my brethren; In the
midst of the assembly I will praise Thee. . . . All the
ends of the earth will remember and turn to the Lord,
And all the families of the nations will worship before
Thee" (verses 22 and 27).

Micah, who spoke of the king from everlasting, saw
him beaten as a despised outcast: "With a rod they will
smite the judge of Israel on the cheek" (Micah 5:1).

To be slapped on the cheek was the height of insult,
and to be hit with a club was to degrade the sufferer
beyond words. An insulted deliverer? A degraded king?

In the coming One, the priesthood with its offerings
and the throne of Israel would come together. The
priesthood with its bloody sacrifices pointed to a

41

substitute Messiah, while the glorious reign of David foreshadowed His rule over the company that His sacrifice redeemed. It is doubtful that any priest gave a moment's thought to what would happen to his office, or to Judaism, when Messiah came. They were ministers of a temporary and passing system that was a shadow of the substance yet to come.

When the Messiah came, all the prophets joined to say that He would bring an end to sin, and therefore cause sacrifice to cease. The endless blood sacrifices in the hands of the priests were only there because sin had not yet been dealt with. The coming of Messiah would end sacrifice and that would bring the existing priestly office to a close.

The existing priestly office was limited to one tribe, the tribe of Levi—and within that tribe, to the family of Aaron. They stood as the representatives before the Lord on behalf of their brother Israelites, carrying the nation on the shoulders and heart of the high priest. In the priesthood Israel lived in God's presence and communed with Him.

David saw that at the coronation of Shiloh a new priestly order would come into existence, dispensing with the Levitical priesthood. The new order was of the order of Melchizedek.

> The Lord says to my Lord:
> "Sit at My right hand,
> Until I make Thine enemies a footstool
> for Thy feet."
> The Lord will stretch forth Thy strong
> scepter from Zion, saying,
> "Rule in the midst of Thine enemies."

> Thy people will volunteer freely in the
> day of Thy power;
> In holy array, from the womb of the
> dawn,
> Thy youth are to Thee as the dew.
> The Lord has sworn and will not change
> His mind,
> "Thou art a priest forever
> According to the order of Melchizedek."
>> Psalms 110:1-4

Melchizedek appears briefly on the pages of the Scriptures in the early life of Abraham. Abraham had just returned from rescuing his nephew, Lot, from an invading army. God gave Abraham great help and he returned loaded with the spoils.

Abraham was aware that he would never have had his victory without God's help and at once set about returning his thanks to God. At that time, he met a priest who became one of the strangest characters in the sacred books of the Hebrews:

> Then after his return from the defeat of Chedorlaomer and the kings who were with him, the king of Sodom went out to meet him. ...And Melchizedek king of Salem brought out bread and wine; now he was a priest of God Most High.

> And he blessed him and said, "Blessed be Abram of God Most High, Possessor of heaven and earth; And blessed be God Most High,
> Who has delivered your enemies into your hand."
> And he gave him a tenth of all.
>> Genesis 14:17-20

43

Here was a priesthood that was prior to that of Levi, for at that time Levi had not been born. Abraham paid tithes of his spoils to Melchizedek, and because the seed of Levi was in Abraham at that time, in a manner of speaking, Levi also paid tithes to Melchizedek, thus indicating that the priesthood of the future Levites was to be inferior to this priesthood.

Melchizedek was of the nation of Canaan and was called a priest of the Most High God. The title, *Most High God,* is a title of deity that always speaks of the rule of God over all the nations. This Melchizedek was not a priest just for the nation of Israel, but for the whole world.

Every Levitical priest came with a blood sacrifice in his hand, within a sacred precinct. Melchizedek came with a simple meal of bread and wine, shared with Abraham in the place where they met. A priest without an offering and without a temple!

In recording the event, all references to his father or mother were omitted. To an Israelite there could be no priesthood without genealogy. Every priest held his position and office because he could prove from his genealogy that he was of the tribe of Levi and family of Aaron. *His right to priesthood was in his genealogy.* Melchizedek was a priest who held his position and office without a genealogy, receiving his office directly from God.

After this brief mention the mysterious priest disappears from the Scriptures, with no record of his death. The Levitical priesthood was as transient as the system it upheld and the lives of the priests—temporary priests for the temporary system. But to show that

44

Melchizedek was a shadow of a priesthood that would never end, the Holy Spirit omitted any record of his death.

David, under the direction of the Spirit, saw the coronation of Messiah as His induction to a priesthood that would replace Levi—after the order of Melchizedek. The Messiah would not only bring an end to the sacrifices but introduce a new priesthood that would not be continually offering a blood sacrifice, and that would have no temple or holy place. He would stand in His office not dependent upon a genealogy, but appointed by God because of His holy person. Ordained of God to stand, not for one nation, but on behalf of the whole world. His was the priesthood that would never end, the substance that the transient priesthood of Levi had always shadowed. A priesthood after the order of Melchizedek, without beginning or ending.

4

A Greater King to Come

When David came to the throne of Israel, the national level of worship and faith was at an all-time low. For the most part it had degenerated into an empty form, the performance of rituals, the meaning of which had long since been forgotten. The ark of the covenant had been taken from the holy of holies nearly a century before, and was now in a farmhouse in the hill country, discarded by the nation.

God was everywhere present, but the ark had a unique meaning in Israel's worship. It was the symbolic throne of their Lord God, their true king, and it was the place where the blood was sprinkled and God had said He would commune and fellowship with the nation. To have a holy of holies without an ark and the manifest presence of God was to have a nation without a true king and a religion without vital communion with God. Without the ark, the glory of God had departed from them.

Now, the veil in the tabernacle hid nothing, for there was a vacuum at the center of their worship.

As soon as David became king he understood that he was king under the true king, and was but a pointer, a shadow of the final king, "He whose right it was." One of the first things he determined to do was to bring the ark back to the center of Israel, that his reign might be truly under the direction of God's glory. Without His presence at the center the nation was a hollow shell, its glory an empty dream.

In preparing to bring the ark from the farmhouse, he built a tent on a small hill within Jerusalem called Mount Zion. This action was a drastic and unparalleled break from all that had gone before. The tabernacle, its priests, and sacrifices continued in Gibeah as they had for generations; but the holy of holies, the glory of Israel, was officially at Mount Zion in Jerusalem. This was something quite new in Israel's religious history. David was about to embark on a fellowship and communion with the holy One hitherto undreamed of. It was man in the radiant presence without priest or sacrifice, for they never came to Zion, but stayed in the tabernacle in Gibeah.

It must not be thought that David came arrogantly into the presence of God as if he had no sin. No man had a greater sense of the Lord being his salvation, his strength, and his all than David had. The Psalms record his constant dependence on God for *His* salvation. David did not intend the tent on Zion to be permanent, but rather as a temporary measure until he could build a temple adequate to reflect the greatness of God.

And so the ark of the covenant was brought from the farmhouse into Jerusalem. It was accompanied by joy and praise unique in Israel. David, oblivious of all but the God he delighted in, leaped and spun in holy dance before Him, stopping every few paces for sacrifices.

To David, this was the symbolic entrance of the Lord of glory to take His true place at the center of the nation. Tradition tells us that he wrote Psalm 24 for this great day: "Lift up your heads, O gates, And be lifted up, O ancient doors, That the King of glory may come in!" (verse 7).

From within the city came the answer, "Who is the King of glory?" (verse 8).

And the shout from without: "The Lord strong and mighty, The Lord mighty in battle. Lift up your heads, O gates, And lift them up, O ancient doors, That the King of glory may come in!" (verses 8-9).

The worship that began before the ark in the tent on Zion was unparalleled in praise. Jerusalem, with the ark of the covenant on Zion, began a twenty-four hour celebration that the Lord was their God in the midst of them. In later years, prophets summed it in exultant shouts:

> Shout for joy, O daughter of Zion!
> Shout in triumph, O Israel!
> Rejoice and exult with all your heart,
> O daughter of Jerusalem! ...
> The Lord your God is in your midst,
> A victorious warrior.
> He will exult over you with joy,
> He will be quiet in His love,
> He will rejoice over you with shouts of
> joy.
>
> Zephaniah 3:14, 17

49

> Cry aloud and shout for joy, O inhabitant
> of Zion,
> For great in your midst is the Holy One
> of Israel.
>
> Isaiah 12:6

Jerusalem became known as the city of God. Zion and Jerusalem were referred to as "the holy hill of Zion," "the hill of the Lord," "the mountain of the Lord's house." Israel was referred to as "the daughter of Zion." The Israelites were children of the God who made Himself manifest and dwelt in glory among His people.

The Psalms constantly praised God for His presence in Zion. His presence not only made Jerusalem the city of God, but was like a river making all inside its walls glad and at peace (Psalm 46:4). God's dwelling on earth was the perfection of beauty (Psalm 50:2), the place of His glory (Psalm 87:3), and the joy of the whole earth (Psalm 48:2).

Israel's religion was no longer a meaningless ritual—they now entered into the presence of the holy One. And even in the bringing of the ark to Jerusalem, David had seen that it demanded a holiness of heart and life.

> Who may ascend into the hill of the
> Lord?
> And who may stand in His holy place?
> He who has clean hands and a pure
> heart,
> Who has not lifted up his soul to false-
> hood,
> And has not sworn deceitfully.

50

> He shall receive a blessing from the Lord
> And righteousness from the God of his
> salvation.
>
> Psalms 24:3-5

Their religion had become so vital that David could speak of actual communion and dialogue between himself and God: "I was crying to the Lord with my voice, And He answered me from His holy mountain" (Psalms 3:4).

What was seen in Zion was God's purpose for man throughout all ages:

> For the Lord has chosen Zion;
> He has desired it for His habitation.
> "This is My resting place forever;
> Here will I dwell, for I have desired it.
> I will abundantly bless her provision;
> I will satisfy her needy with bread.
> Her priests also I will clothe with salvation;
> And her godly ones will sing aloud for joy."
>
> Psalms 132:13-16

The ornate temple David had planned never came into being, however, but was given to Solomon to accomplish. This meant that the ark stayed on Zion throughout the reign of David. By the time David died, the understanding of worship as seen on the holy hill was well bedded in the religious mind of the people.

The temple was a marriage of the joyful worship on Zion and the priestly functions of the tabernacle. But although the ark was now once more behind the thick veil—the glory of the Lord beheld only once a year by the high priest—the prophets would never forget Zion, seeing it as a piece of history that was in itself a prophecy of an age to come.

When the Messiah would come and sin would be taken away, then what had been briefly glimpsed in Zion would become a way of life. Zion as a *place* was now derelict—but the *experience* of Zion, its message, was a prophecy of the day when the glory of the Lord would be revealed and men would live in it. The concept of Zion became the foundation of their description of the coming kingdom of Messiah.

Messiah would be the builder of a new temple. When telling David that he could not build the temple, Nathan spoke of the greater descendant than Solomon who would not only reign forever but build a house for the Lord:

> When your days are complete and you lie down with your fathers, I will raise up your descendant after you, who will come forth from you, and I will establish his kingdom.
> He shall build a house for My name, and I will establish the throne of his kingdom forever.
> 2 Samuel 7:12-13

The prophets spoke of the coming kingdom over which the son of David would reign as the renewal of the worship as seen on Zion. Not a revival of the constant bloodshedding and changing priesthood of Solomon's temple on Moriah, but the holy joy of Zion—without priest, without blood being constantly shed. Amos spoke boldly of the day when the tent of David would be rebuilt: "In that day I will raise up the fallen booth of David, And wall up its breaches; I will also raise up its ruins, And rebuild it as in the days of old" (Amos 9:11).

A much later prophet, Zechariah, had a vision describing a Jerusalem of the future: "In that day there will be inscribed on the bells of the horses, 'HOLY TO THE LORD.' And the cooking pots in the Lord's house will be like the bowls before the altar. And every cooking pot in Jerusalem and in Judah will be holy to the Lord of hosts" (Zechariah 14:20-21). The expression "Holy to the Lord" was the inscription on the miter of the high priest who alone could enter the presence and stand in the glory before the ark.

Zechariah saw a day when the secular Jeru-salem— at business, driving through the streets, cooking in the kitchen—would be *inscribed as those who lived within the veil.* To such people all was spiritual. It was to be a day when the dichotomy between secular and spiritual was done away and all of life would be lived in the glory of God.

Not only was the Messiah seen as the architect of the Zion of the future day, but also His coronation would take place in Zion: "But as for Me, I have installed My King Upon Zion, My holy mountain. I will surely tell of the decree of the Lord: He said to Me, 'Thou art My Son, Today I have begotten Thee'" (Psalms 2:6-7). The One the ark of the covenant had ever spoken of would come to Zion and be crowned king of the earth. From there He would extend His reign over the whole earth: "'Ask of Me, and I will surely give the nations as Thine inheritance, And the very ends of the earth as Thy possession. Thou shalt break them with a rod of iron, Thou shalt shatter them like earthenware' " (Psalms 2:8-9).

The prophets spoke of Zion in its spiritual and highest sense. They no longer saw it as a geographical location on a hill within Jerusalem, but rather as a *state of being* that was best described by all that had been historically witnessed in Zion: *God and man in joyful unity.*

Describing the kingdom of Messiah, Isaiah saw it as all nations coming to the holy mountain. That could never happen if the geographical location was spoken of:

> In the last days, The mountain of the house of the Lord
> Will be established as the chief of the mountains,
> And will be raised above the hills;
> And all the nations will stream to it.
> And many peoples will come and say,
> "Come, let us go up to the mountain of the Lord,
> To the house of the God of Jacob;
> That He may teach us concerning His ways,
> And that we may walk in His paths."
> For the law will go forth from Zion,
> And the word of the Lord from Jerusalem.
>
> Isaiah 2:2-3

Isaiah describes the nations that come to Zion as eager in the anticipation of learning God's law. These had once been aligned to Satan, hating God's law; now they love His law and desire to know it. These are people with a changed nature who enthusiastically converge on the rule of the Messiah to submit themselves to Him.

> And He will judge between the nations,
> And will render decisions for many peoples;
> And they will hammer their swords into plowshares,
> And their spears into pruning hooks.
> Nation will not lift up sword against nation,
> And never again will they learn war.
>
> Isaiah 2:4

Nations that would normally be fighting among themselves do so no more. Their coming under the reign of the king in Zion has caused them to transform their weapons into implements to bring forth fruit and bless each other. Within that kingdom people live under God's king, side by side in love. *His kingdom is made up of many nations dwelling together in the state of being called Zion.* They are a pocket of love and peace in a world of strife and destruction.

But Zion was not only a state of indescribable peace, but also of joy that had been seen in David as he leaped and danced on his way to Jerusalem at the establishment of the historical geographical Zion.

> And the ransomed of the Lord will
> return,
>> And come with joyful shouting to Zion,
>> With everlasting joy upon their heads.
>> They will find gladness and joy,
>> And sorrow and sighing will flee away.
>>> Isaiah 35:10

Everlasting joy is a joy without beginning or ending. Anything so eternal can be true only of God. Here is God's joy, that has no beginning or ending, being infused into people. God is its end even as He is its source. No fortune can bring it, any more than misfortune can destroy it.

Isaiah sees the ransomed company coming, those who once had been blind, deaf, and lame, now dancing with joy down the way of holiness to Zion: "Then the eyes of the blind will be opened, And the ears of the deaf will be unstopped. Then the lame will leap like a deer, And the tongue of the dumb will shout for joy" (Isaiah 35:5-6).

The way will be so simple that no one can miss it, and nothing will be on the highway to hinder those who find it: "And a highway will be there, a roadway, And it will be called 'the highway of holiness.' The unclean will not travel on it, But it will be for him who walks that way, And fools will not wander on it" (Isaiah 35:8).

It is doubtful that the prophets understood all they were saying, let alone its implications. How could Zion be a state of being, yet at the same time be a reigning king who had to be turned to? How could all nations be included in a day of Israel's glory? How could there be a nation made of all nations?

They wrote and pondered and waited for the last days of the era in which they lived, knowing that, at the end of those days, Messiah would come and His glorious kingdom would burst forth on the earth.

5

Judgment on Israel

The prophets announced the kingdom that would spring from the nation of Israel and be ruled over by the Lord's Messiah. They described its beauty, and how love, joy, peace, and righteousness would hold absolute sway.

In 770 B.C., such words sounded arrogant and the height of the most idealistic foolishness. The mammoth nation of Assyria had its own ideas as to the nature of the world empire of the future. Already its cruel armies had eaten up the smaller surrounding nations in its bid for universal power. For a small nation such as Israel, already torn by civil war and on the decrease in power, to talk of a future glorious world kingdom was like a mouse announcing to a herd of elephants its plans to rule over them.

Where did the idealistic dream of a world kingdom of love fit into the cold facts of a world under the control of the wicked one? Where did

Messiah's kingdom fit into a theater of bloodshed, lust for power and all its attendant sorrows?

The prophets and psalmists looked the world scene squarely in the eye and sang of their Most High God who reigned over all the ragings of men. Although the rebellion was in full sway, the prophets, with bold and audacious faith, reminded Israel that the same breath with which they cursed God was given them by God. The rebellion was taking place inside His rule. He was still the Most High.

At man's puny rebellion God laughed. He would establish His kingdom in Zion in spite of all who raged against Him:

> The kings of the earth take their stand,
> And the rulers take counsel together
> Against the Lord and against His Anointed:
> "Let us tear their fetters apart,
> And cast away their cords from us!"
> He who sits in the heavens laughs,
> The Lord scoffs at them.
> Then He will speak to them in His anger
> And terrify them in His fury:
> "But as for Me, I have installed My king
> Upon Zion, My holy mountain."
>
> Psalms 2:2-6

Assyria seemed such a threat, but in the hand of God it was a weapon of His judgment. The Lord who reigned over the rebellion of Assyria was using the pride and lust of that nation to achieve His end and prepare the way for the coming One.

60

Israel need not sit back smugly depending on a genealogy that went back to Abraham. The ax would fall on them, the cedars of Lebanon in God's forest. They had, by their rebellion, relinquished their right to the promises.

But not all was lost, for not all of Israel was the Israel of faith. A remnant still held faith, and after the judgment on the *nation* the remnant would return to the land and prepare for the fulfillment of God's promises: "A remnant will return, the remnant of Jacob, to the mighty God. For though your people, O Israel, may be like the sand of the sea, Only a remnant within them will return" (Isaiah 10:21-22).

The nation that had been the beauty of the earth under David and Solomon was now a stump on the forest floor, a remnant of the tree. Out of that remnant that would return there, however, would spring a shoot centered in the descendant of David:

> Then a shoot will spring from the stem of Jesse,
> And a branch from his roots will bear fruit.
> And the Spirit of the Lord will rest on Him,
> The spirit of wisdom and understanding,
> The spirit of counsel and strength,
> The spirit of knowledge and the fear of the Lord.
> And He will delight in the fear of the Lord,
> And He will not judge by what His eyes see,

Nor make a decision by what His ears hear;

But with righteousness He will judge the poor,

And decide with fairness for the afflicted of the ear;

And He will strike the earth with the rod of His mouth,

And with the breath of His lips He will slay the wicked.

Also righteousness will be the belt about His loins,

And faithfulness the belt about His waist.

Isaiah 11:1-5

The old Israelite nation would be dead, cut off in judgment. Out of its stump would come a new tree, a new nation, a new Israel—life from the dead. That life would be centered in one person, the descendant of David. Israel was to find its focus, not in its glory as a nation, but in one person to whom all nations would come and find rest: "And it shall be in that day that the Root of Jesse shall stand for a signal to the peoples; of Him shall the nations inquire and seek knowledge, and His dwelling shall be glory—His rest glorious!" (Isaiah 11:10, AMP).

As the prophets had said, the Assyrians came. They swallowed up the northern half of the divided nation and harassed the south where the family of David still reigned. Assyria fell finally to Babylon, and Nebuchadnezzar, King of Babylon, turned his sights to the little kingdom of Judah that teetered on the edge of collapse.

Within Jerusalem in those fear-filled days Jeremiah prophesied, explaining and enlarging what Isaiah had said before him. He saw Babylon as God's agent to bring judgment on the nation that had forsaken Him. The cedar of Lebanon was about to be cut down to a stump. But there would be a return:

> Therefore thus says the Lord of hosts,...
>
> "I will send to Nebuchadnezzar king of Babylon, My servant, and will bring them against this land, and against its inhabitants ... and I will utterly destroy them, and make them a horror, and a hissing, and an everlasting desolation.
>
> "Moreover, I will take from them the voice of joy and the voice of gladness, the voice of the bridegroom and the voice of the bride, the sound of the millstones and light of the lamp.
>
> "And this whole land shall be a desolation and a horror, and these nations shall serve the king of Babylon seventy years."
>
> Jeremiah 25:8-11

Seventy years—and then those Isaiah had designated as the remnant would be free to return. Jeremiah foresaw that day in vivid words:

> "Again I will build you, and you shall be rebuilt,
> O virgin of Israel!
> Again you shall take up your tambourines,

63

And go forth to the dances of the merry-
makers.
Again you shall plant vineyards
On the hills of Samaria;
The planters shall plant
And shall enjoy them.
For there shall be a day when watchmen
On the hills of Ephraim shall call out,
'Arise, and let us go up to Zion,
To the Lord our God.'"

Hear the word of the Lord, O nations,
And declare in the coastlands afar off,
And say, "He who scattered Israel will
gather him,
And keep him as a shepherd keeps his
flock."
For the Lord has ransomed Jacob,
And redeemed him from the hand of him
who was stronger than he.
"And they shall come and shout for joy
on the height of Zion,
And they shall be radiant over the bounty
of the Lord—
Over the grain, and the new wine, and
the oil,
And over the young of the flock and the
herd;
And their life shall be like a watered
garden,
And they shall never languish again.
Then the virgin shall rejoice in the
dance,
And the young men and the old, to-
gether;
For I will turn their mourning into joy,

And will comfort them, and give them
joy for their sorrow.
And I will fill the soul of the priests with
abundance,
And My people shall be satisfied with
My goodness," declares the Lord.

Jeremiah 31:4-6, 10-14

Jeremiah went on to identify these days of
return with the making of the new covenant that
would deal with the sin problem forever (Jeremiah
31:31 and verses following). But the people within
Jerusalem as a whole did not hear his words, and
after a bitter struggle Nebuchadnezzar carried his
captives to Babylon, leaving Jerusalem a smoking
ruin.

The Israelite slaves carried with them their holy
books, and established places of prayer where they
read them each week. The cry for Messiah to come
became a sob in the hearts of the captives. Their
pagan neighbors observed and listened—and
within the next two hundred years He who was the
hope of Israel became the desire of many nations.

Among the original captives that were carried
in chains across the desert were two young men
who were to see the final stages of the setting up
of Messiah's kingdom among the nations of the
world. One was Daniel, the other Ezekiel.

Daniel was unmoved by the collapse of his
nation and calmly acknowledged that it was God's
doing. He rapidly moved through the schools of
Babylon and became one of the wise men of the
city—an interpreter of events to the king. When
Nebuchadnezzar had a dream, it was the task of

the wise men to interpret its meaning. So it was presented to Daniel one day to discover a dream that Nebuchadnezzar had and then to interpret it. The impossible task was accomplished with a word of wisdom and a word of knowledge. He recorded it in the second chapter of his prophecy.

The interpretation was the outline of history down to the last days of the era in which they lived. It was God's announcement, made in the heart of the world's camp, that He finally controlled history. In the boiling pot of nations, as they rose and fell, men tearing each other apart in their grasp for power, God quietly achieved His purposes and brought about His kingdom.

Babylon now ruled on a world scale, but it was not to rule forever. Babylon would be followed by others: "And after you there will rise another kingdom inferior to you, then another third kingdom of bronze, which will rule over all the earth" (Daniel 2:39).

Daniel didn't know the names of those kingdoms, but we have seen their path through history as the Medo-Persian empire, followed by Alexander the Great and the Greeks.

The fourth empire, a nation of iron, cruel and powerful, would swallow up all that had gone before. That nation we know as Rome, the nation that held peace across the world by its force as none other ever had. But it was not a peace such as the Prince of Peace would bring, for men do not mix with men when all crave their own way. Rome would be a nation with a faulty foundation.

Each nation had been swallowed up by the one previous to it. Rome was a conglomerate of

Babylon, Persia, and Greece—apart from its own originality that brought it to history. So Daniel went on to say:

> And in the days of those kings the God of heaven will set up a kingdom which will never be destroyed, and that kingdom will not be left for another people; it will crush and put an end to all these kingdoms, but it will itself endure forever.
>
> Inasmuch as you saw that a stone was cut out of the mountain without hands and that it crushed the iron, the bronze, the clay, the silver, and the gold, the great God has made known to the king what will take place in the future; so the dream is true, and its interpretation is trustworthy.
>
> Daniel 2:44-45

The new kingdom did not inherit from its predecessor ,but came from the outside, smashing all of man's rule and glory. It had no glory that the man of the image would be impressed with—just a stone cut without hands, and small at that. But that stone was destined to fill the whole earth, and Daniel called it the kingdom of God.

It was the promise of Genesis 3 fully explained. Each successive nation was the serpent rearing its head, spitting out rebellion at God's authority. Each king or dictator craved omnipotence and sovereignty—the hiss of the serpent come of age: "You will be like God."

Daniel saw further visions of the world empires that were coming and of the kingdom that would finally replace them. He saw in detail the coronation that David had referred to in Psalm 2.

> I kept looking in the night visions,
> And behold, with the clouds of heaven
> One like a Son of Man was coming,
> And He came up to the Ancient of Days
> And was presented before Him.
> And to Him was given dominion,
> Glory and a kingdom,
> That all the peoples, nations, and men of
> every language
> Might serve Him.
> His dominion is an everlasting dominion
> Which will not pass away;
> And His kingdom is one
> Which will not be destroyed.
> Daniel 7:13-14

The throne from which Messiah would rule the world would be no earthly throne, but in the heavens. The throne of David on earth was only an earthly shadow of the throne in heaven to be occupied by *Shiloh*.

Daniel groped for words in his description. Obviously what he was seeing was very real, but he was at a loss for words in human vocabulary to describe it. The Zion where the Lord would crown His Anointed was not an earthly city but in a heavenly dimension. From a throne that was beyond the time-space dimension, Messiah would rule all nations.

Then Zion of peace, righteousness, and love— to which all nations would come with dancing and great joy—was in a heavenly dimension, too. This by no means makes it unreal, existing only in the minds of those who choose to believe it. Here was a very objective Zion—but invisible, and its throne in the heavens. The things that are seen are already passing away; it is the invisible that is eternally real.

Back in Israel, Jerusalem, the city of Zion with the throne of David, was a heap of ruins covered with dust and decay. Foxes prowled where David once danced, and owls hooted where Levites had sung. But Daniel saw the reality of which that had been the shadow. Here was the Zion that could not pass, a center of rule, and a king that would be forever.

Although the darkest hour in captive Israel's history, it was their greatest hour of faith. While nations laughed at God and planned their glory, the prophets proclaimed with the audacity of faith that God's kingdom would be established. The Lord would gather His aching people and establish Zion.

6

Seed of the Spirit

The captivity ended as the prophets had foreseen, and a minority of the nation of Israel returned to the land of their fathers. Left among the nations of the world were thousands of Jews who became Greek-speaking. They translated the Old Testament into Greek and so put the prophecies of the coming Messiah into the hands of the whole world. The term, *Messiah*, was on every Hebrew lip; and its Greek equivalent, *Christ*, was the discussion of tens of thousands of their Gentile neighbors.

The centuries that followed the return from captivity were a dense religious darkness. The nations had tired under bloodshed and conquest and turned away, searching for a reality beyond the mundane. They searched with their reason, and philosophers talked and wrote of wisdom; but their reasoning was based on the lie and left man in a greater darkness than before. The philosophers soared to the height of human reason, but left men unsure about God, the universe, and themselves. The occult flourished, stirring the emotions of the masses left cold by the philosophers. Magic and witchcraft held other masses captive in a mental and spiritual darkness.

In the midst of the spiritual night the Jews were pinpoints of light and truth as they expounded from the Law and the prophets of the coming deliverer. Gentiles were converted and entered the synagogue to wait with them.

Sadly, the vast majority of the Jews missed the main thrust of what Messiah was coming to do. They passed the promises through the grill of their fierce nationalism and came out with a distorted picture quite different from the message of the prophets as a whole.

They wanted and spoke in hushed tones of the Messiah, the Christ, the hope of Israel who would bring the Gentile nations of the world to their knees and establish His glorious Israel that every Jew had dreamed of since David's reign. It would be a glorious conquest that would wipe out the aggressor and bring in a golden age with the Jew as lord of the earth.

The Jews had missed the thrust of the prophecies that the kingdom the Lord's Anointed would set up was one of righteousness, love, and a peace that could only be when self-centeredness had died—a kingdom overflowing with a joy that was not in possessing things, but in possessing God Himself. Above all, they missed the fact that the Israel of Messiah was to be made up of all nations, one nation under Christ, and not a matter of Abraham's physical seed but of his faith.

For centuries the prophets had recognized that not all the members of the visible defined nation of Israel were to be recipients of the promise. They constantly spoke of a community within the whole known only to God and called *the remnant.*

The identity of the recipients of the promise made to Abraham is of the greatest importance. The promises were made to Abraham *and his seed—not seeds,* therefore to discover the seed is to discover the recipient and object of the promise. Who is, and what constitutes, the seed of Abraham?

At the very beginning, when God promised Abraham that through him all nations would be blessed, it became evident that *the seed of Abraham to whom the promises were made and through whom they would be fulfilled was never to be understood as all those who had his blood in their veins.*

Before Isaac's birth Abraham had hoped that Ishmael, his son by Hagar, would be the son of promise. He was told plainly that the covenant promises would not come through Ishmael, but through a son yet to be born—Isaac: ". . . for through Isaac your descendants shall be named" (Genesis 21:12).

Later Abraham had many sons by another wife, Keturah, but none of them were given the covenant promise and none of them responded with covenant faith.

> . . . neither are they all children because they are Abraham's descendants, but: "THROUGH ISAAC YOUR DESCENDANTS WILL BE NAMED." *That is, it is not the children of the*

> *flesh who are children of God, but the*
> *children of the promise are regarded as*
> *descendants.*
> Romans 9:7-8 (author's italics)

Jacob and Esau were a further narrowing down of what was meant by the seed of Abraham; it was Jacob who was chosen as the one through whom the covenant should be established.

Out of Jacob came the twelve tribes known as the nation of Israel. As a nation they bore the title of the seed of Abraham: "But you, Israel, My servant, Jacob whom I have chosen, Descendant of Abraham My friend" (Isaiah 41:8). They were the visible seed— possessors and guardians of the promises that spoke of salvation. But their being heirs of the promises and their enjoying the privileges of God's covenant people were conditional upon their keeping the covenant: "God said further to Abraham, 'Now as for you, you shall keep My covenant, you and your descendants after you throughout their generations'" (Genesis 17:9).

The prophets recognized that the covenants and promises were not made to those who merely had Abraham's blood, *even if they were part of the visible community of Israel.* The covenant was to those who shared the *faith* of Abraham and so kept the covenant. Their messages to the people narrowed the ultimate fulfilling of the promise even further to a community within Israel.

They warned the people that if there was no loyalty to the covenant there could be no national continuance. The judgment and captivity were because of the broken covenant. But they looked

74

through the gloom of judgment and spoke of a *remnant* who would ultimately inherit the promise made to Abraham. The seed of Abraham was seen as a remnant within the nation: "A remnant will return, the remnant of Jacob, to the mighty God. For though your people, O Israel, may be like the sand of the sea, Only a remnant within them will return . . ." (Isaiah 10:21-22).

The concept is summed in Romans 9:6-8:

> For they are not all Israel who are descended from Israel;
> neither are they all children because they are Abraham's descendants, but: "THROUGH ISAAC YOUR DESCENDANTS WILL BE NAMED."
> That is, it is not the children of the flesh who are children of God, but the children of the promise are regarded as descendants.

The proud spirit of Judaism was crushed one more time when Rome took over the divided Greek empire. Israel had an oppressor more cruel and demanding than all that had gone before. History was entering on the era of the legs of iron.

7

"A Virgin Shall Conceive"

Four hundred years had elapsed since Malachi had prophesied of the Sun of Righteousness rising into the darkness of man's sin. A remnant looked beyond the hate and prayed for Messiah to come. It was the hope of every mother in Judah that hers would be the Anointed One, for the time of His coming was now according to Daniel's ancient prophecy.

The temple became the center to which the faithful who saw the spiritual nature of the kingdom gravitated. Anna, an old prophetess who had spent over half a century in prayer, was a regular figure in the temple courtyard. She spoke to all who had ears to hear of the Christ who was to come at any time. Another was Simeon, often seen around the temple precincts, who confidently stated that the coming of Messiah was so close that he would not see death until the hope of Israel had come.

The priesthood was a mixture. The high priest family was sold out to the politics of their position. They continued the thinking of the people and played a game of roulette with the current Roman procurator, who vainly sought to keep the seething patriotism under control.

Hundreds of priests went unthinkingly through the ritual and sacrifice, glad to go home at the end of the day. A few looked beyond the sacrifices as well as the politics and looked for the Christ.

One such priest was Zacharias. He resided with his wife, Elizabeth, in the lonely hill country of Judah when not engaged in his priestly duties in Jerusalem. They had no child, and all hope of having one had long since been given up. It was a shame to be childless in Israel, and even more so when all mothers looked upon their male children as potential Messiahs.

One day, in the exercise of his duty, the old man left the multitude of people and went on their behalf into the holy place to offer incense. As he entered, he saw an angel standing on the right side of the altar of incense. As a priest, he was well familiar with religious objects, but he melted with fear at a glimpse of the reality of the supernatural. The angel's voice broke the silence:

> "Do not be afraid, Zacharias, for your petition has been heard, and your wife Elizabeth will bear you a son, and you will give him the name John.
>
> "And you will have joy and gladness, and many will rejoice at his birth.

> "For he will be great in the sight of the Lord, and he will drink no wine or liquor; and he will be filled with the Holy Spirit, while yet in his mother's womb.
>
> "And he will turn back many of the sons of Israel to the Lord their God.
>
> "And it is he who will go as a forerunner before Him in the spirit and power of Elijah, to turn the hearts of the fathers back to the children, and the disobedient to the attitude of the righteous; so as to make ready a people prepared for the Lord."
>
> Luke 1:13-17

It was the first word from God for nearly four hundred years. The breaking of the silence took up exactly where the last words of Malachi had ended: "Behold, I am going to send you Elijah the prophet before the coming of the great and terrible day of the Lord. And he will restore the hearts of the fathers to their children, and the hearts of the children to their fathers, lest I come and smite the land with a curse" (Malachi 4:5-6).

Before the day of God would burst on man and deal with sin, one would come who would be as Elijah had been. Messiah would have a herald who would be a voice lifted up in the darkness of a pagan world and a nationalistic Israel. The people would be called to see the true nature of the kingdom before the king came.

The forerunner of Messiah was about to be born— his name would be "John."

Zacharias hesitated. It was ridiculous. He thought of his aged wife who had bid him goodbye a couple of days ago. He tried to imagine her

79

swollen with child and would have laughed but for his terror. Such things belonged in the holy books with the stories of Sarah and Rebekah. He looked at the angel and said, "How shall I know this for certain? For I am an old man, and my wife is advanced in years" (Luke 1:18).

The angel's answering words struck fear into Zacharias: "I am Gabriel, who stands in the presence of God; and I have been sent to speak to you, and to bring you this good news. And behold, you shall be silent and unable to speak until the day when these things take place, because you did not believe my words, which shall be fulfilled in their proper time" (Luke 1:19-20).

The angel was gone, and Zacharias staggered dumbly to the door and the restless waiting people. The terror in his eyes, his flaying arms, and his dumb mouth told them he had confronted the supernatural. Junior priests helped him away.

Within the month Elizabeth was pregnant.

The young girl stood awestruck before the presence that filled the room with light that was at once terrifying and beautiful. She heard words she could hardly believe: "Hail, favored one! The Lord is with you" (Luke 1:28).

Outside, Nazareth went on its way as it had for generations. Donkeys carried the loads of rich men through the narrow streets. Merchants haggled in the streetside shops over the price of goods. Shepherds stood at the well and swapped stories as their sheep were watered. Old men sucked on toothless gums in the market place and spat at the Roman soldiers who marched arrogantly by, the

ever-present reminder that Israel was an occupied
nation under the iron heel of Rome. Young
members of the zealot underground movement sat
in back kitchens planning to kill the centurion who
had ordered the crucifixion of their fellow Israelites,
who even now hung naked on bloodstained
crosses on the hills outside Jerusalem.

And in that little room in Nazareth, the hopes
and prophecies of generations were about to be
fulfilled. Words that had hung fresh on the air since
the dawn of history were now to become concrete
fact.

The angel continued to speak:

> Do not be afraid, Mary; for you have
> found favor with God.
> And behold, you will conceive in your
> womb, and bear a son, and you shall name
> Him JESUS.
> He will be great, and will be called the
> Son of the Most High; and the Lord God will
> give Him the throne of His father David;
> and He will reign over the house of
> Jacob forever; and His kingdom will have no
> end.
>
> Luke 1:30-33

The words were strangely familiar to her ears.
She had heard them, or words like them, ever since
she could remember. They were as familiar as the
crooning songs her mother had sung to her in the
cradle. The promise of the deliverer, the king who
would reign forever over Israel in glorious reign,
was told to every Israelite. Mary had heard it more
than the average Israelite girl, for she was one of

the remaining descendants of king David. But for the Roman occupation, she would have been of royal status.

Mary had been taught since childhood that she was part of the family of David that was now a dead stump in the forest of the nations. They had been so for centuries. But they waited for the goal of the prophecy that had gone on to speak of the One promised to David. It said that a shoot would spring out of the dead stump, and the One that all nations waited for, and all history revolved around, would be born. The Spirit would be upon Him and He would reign, bringing about a kingdom of unbelievable and everlasting peace.

The words that hung on the air of the glory-filled room in Nazareth said that, in her, He would come and ascend the throne of David and reign forever. He whose right it had always been had finally come, and the scepter would never depart, the throne never passed to another. He would reign over God's Israel forever.

Such familiar words the angel spoke did not strike her as strange. What sent a thrill of fear and unease was that they were spoken to *her*—that she would now conceive and bear a son. For she was not married, only engaged to Joseph, the carpenter in the marketplace who also was a descendant of David through another branch of the family.

"How can this be, since I am a virgin?" she asked hesitantly (Luke 1:34).

"The Holy Spirit will come upon you, and the power of the Most High will overshadow you; and for that reason the holy offspring shall be called the Son of God," replied the angel (Luke 1:35).

The words echoed dizzily around the young girl's head as the angel continued, "And behold, even your relative Elizabeth has also conceived a son in her old age; and she who was called barren is now in her sixth month. For nothing will be impossible with God" (Luke 1:36-37).

The words were beyond her understanding. She could not grasp their full significance, but she bowed to the messenger and said, "Behold, the bond-slave of the Lord; be it done to me according to your word" (Luke 1:38).

Suddenly the room was empty. The words of the angel were settled in Mary's mind now, even though she did not understand. Something had happened in her body. But how could she explain to Joseph, or to anyone, what she didn't understand herself? Nothing that had happened in the last hours fitted a category in her mind—a pregnant girl who had never known a man, a wild tale of a visit from an angel with an announcement of fulfilled prophecy that a universal ruler was to be born. Who would believe her!

One word of the angel's message, however, related to her tangible world: "Your relative Elizabeth." Mary remembered her. An old lady—she seemed very old to the young girl's vague memory of the last time she had seen her. She had the vague recollection of woman talk that old Elizabeth had never been able to have children—and the angel had said that she was now six months pregnant! Elizabeth was a link in the tangible world with what the angel had said. Mary knew she must go to her.

The hill country of Judah where Zacharias and Elizabeth lived was hard to get to. Mary was tired as she came in through the door and greeted Elizabeth—greeted her with anticipated joy—for she saw that she was pregnant, and she now knew for certain that she was also.

As she greeted Elizabeth, the elderly woman raised her hands and spoke in a loud voice and prophesied:

> "Blessed among women are you, and blessed is the fruit of your womb!
>
> "And how has it happened to me, that the mother of my Lord should come to me?
>
> "For behold, when the sound of your greeting reached my ears, the baby leaped in my womb for joy.
>
> "And blessed is she who believed that there would be a fulfillment of what had been spoken to her by the Lord."
>
> Luke 1:42-45

As she spoke, the Holy Spirit came upon Mary and she suddenly knew and understood as never before. She could see the end of God's purposes from the beginning. She now saw who this One was within her—none other than the offspring of Abraham, the One promised from the beginning of the Israelite nation. A holy joy welled in her spirit and she began to praise God with a golden tongue. *The promises that the whole world should be blessed were made to the One whom she carried in her womb.*

Israel was about to become all that God meant it to be! All that the Lord had ever called Israel to be, all that Israel had ever been promised—*all* was wrapped up in that One. And when He was born, all nations would be blessed. A universal kingdom centered in that blessed One would radiate blessing to a world that lay under the curse of sin. Deliverance from all enemies and the shackles of Satan.

Mary stayed with Elizabeth for three months, and then returned home, obviously pregnant, to tell Joseph. She could not fault his reaction, his decision to put her away secretly. Why should he believe her and her story of angelic visitation, a child fathered by the Holy Spirit, or of miracles performed in the hills of Judea?

She lay sobbing on her bed trying to piece together the events of the months since the angel had come from the other world with the message of the king to be born. Surely, if the One in her womb was to bring eternal blessedness, why was it that her pillow was soaked with tears?

But while Joseph was thinking about what he should do, he was visited by an angel of the Lord in a dream. The message was simple and to the point:

> "Joseph, son of David, do not be afraid to take Mary as your wife; for that which has been conceived in her is of the Holy Spirit.
> "And she will bear a Son; and you shall call His name Jesus, for it is He who will save His people from their sins."
> Matthew 1:20-21

The months flew by. The talk in Nazareth buzzed louder as the pregnant girl made her way to the well each morning, carrying the child that everyone knew was not

Joseph's. It was a difficult time for both of them, for only they and Elizabeth knew the truth about the child Mary carried in her womb.

8

The Promise Kept

Mary and Joseph were aware that the baby developing in her womb was the promised One, but beyond that it was all they could do to cope with the unfolding situation.

They were not students of the Law or the prophets, but peasants living quietly in Nazareth until their lives were disrupted by the recent events. They were not directors of a drama, but actors in it. They were not making up a script to fit ancient prophecies, but had been caught up in the drama—a drama written before the foundation of the world and directed by the Holy Spirit.

In the whirlwind of events, they had no time or bent of mind to consider that Micah had prophesied seven centuries ago that Messiah must be born in Bethlehem. With only weeks left before the birth of the baby, they were in Nazareth, with no plans for moving.

The Most High rules over all the nations, and, in and through them, achieves His purpose. He chose a heathen emperor to bring to pass His greatest purpose. Across the seas, in the Roman court, Augustus Caesar decided to conduct a census throughout his empire with a view to higher taxation. In Israel the method of the census was that every man return to his tribe and city of ancestry so his family could be counted. Since both Mary and Joseph were direct descendants of David the king, they would have to return to Bethlehem, the family home of the royal line.

The news of the censure was received with a mixture of joy and distress. With the baby due in a few weeks such a journey was not relished. Only Mary's royal descent would necessitate her going. But for all the discomfort of such a trek, it would be a welcome relief from Nazareth's gossip and despising stares. In all likelihood, they set out for Bethlehem in late March or early April.

The village of Bethlehem was about seventy miles south, a two-day journey at most. But, in all probability, they made the journey much longer by going along the banks of the Jordan River to avoid the Samaritans.

About four days after setting out from Nazareth, dusty and travel-worn, the couple arrived in sight of Bethlehem. The hills of the wilderness were purple in the dusk as the Lord and descendant of David in the womb of Mary passed through the gates. They were there by order of a pagan oppressor that the Messiah, ruler of the universe, might be born in Bethlehem as Micah the Prophet had said.

The city was overflowing with travelers. Every home and lodging place was filled to capacity. The couple was glad to find rest in a cave where animals were stabled.

Outside the town, shepherds watched over their sheep. They were not ordinary shepherds, for the rabbinical Law forbade the keeping of flocks in the vicinity of a city or town. Ordinary flocks would be found in wilderness areas only. The only flocks that would be found in the vicinity of Jerusalem and Bethlehem were temple flocks bred exclusively for sacrifice at the Passover. The Law spoke of them as being in the fields at least a month prior to Passover, and so we can be fairly certain that it was in late March that the couple settled into the stable cave. They would register with the authorities tomorrow and then stay until the birth of their child.

It was a few nights later that the temple shepherds were arrested by the sky opening and myriad angels bursting into view. The glory of the Lord lit up the fields, and the angel of the Lord said to them:

> "Do not be afraid; for behold, I bring you good news of a great joy which shall be for all the people;
>
> "For today in the city of David there has been born for you a Savior, who is Christ the Lord.
>
> "And this will be a sign for you: you will find a baby wrapped in cloths, and lying in a manger."
>
> Luke 2:10-12

89

The Lord Messiah, the Savior and blesser of the world, was born. The sign they were to look for was the most amazing of all: the Christ who was to rule the world lying in a manger.

Just as suddenly as the glory had burst upon them, it departed. All was as before. The stars winked in the velvet black sky above, tall grasses bent before the cold breeze on a nearby ridge, and the only sound was the bleating of the nearby sheep.

But the angel *had* been there. The heavenly choir *had* sung, and everyone had clearly heard the message: Messiah was born in Bethlehem tonight in a stable cave. They left the flocks and ran to the town.

The young mother listened to the bright-eyed, rough-speaking men who babbled their story. Their words fitted what she had been told by the heavenly messenger, and she filed it away in her puzzled mind.

The shepherds went through the streets telling everyone who cared to hear. By the following night even the people in nearby Jerusalem were gathered in clusters, discussing the shepherds' story that had come to them from Bethlehem. Simeon and Anna worshiped God. A new day was dawning, the first light of the Sun of Righteousness was appearing in the darkness.

The Messiah was a baby, born of a human mother. As Isaiah had said, "For a child will be born to us." But He was more than a child born—Isaiah had also said, "a son will be given to us" (Isaiah 9:6). Here was One born who was the gift of God, out of God Himself, One who always had existed.

Micah, who had seen this birth in Bethlehem, had said that this babe's going forth was from eternity. Eternity, without beginning. The unbeginning God has experienced beginning in this child lying in the manger. This One was utterly different from all other children, even though completely one with them. *He chose to be born.* The eternal I AM, forever existing, chose to enter the process of beginning an existence.

Not that the babe was aware of who He was. The choice that the eternal God had made was to become a true man, beginning as a true baby. He who knew all things chose to enter a babyhood that knew nothing, and had to learn line upon line. God had taken the style of a servant: the mentality first of a baby, then a boy, a teenager, and finally a man.

That babe was greater than all men, all worlds. He was the man who was God, among us to finally glorify His name, save men, and destroy the lie forever.

The young mother who nursed her babe that night was the one who should be saying what the first mother had said, "I have gotten a man—the Lord" (*see* Genesis 4:1, margin), for she was the virgin who had conceived, and her child was God with us.

They named Him Jesus, as the angel had told Mary before His birth. The name was added to the official family rolls of the tribe of Judah. His family roll carried the names of the kings of Judah back to David and before that to Abraham. Although He was truly God, He was truly man, with a place among the families of men.

In Jerusalem, Simeon had long awaited the Messiah, the hope of Israel. He had been assured by the Holy Spirit that he would not see death until he had seen the Lord's Anointed. One morning, he was aware that the Spirit was urging him to the temple. He moved rapidly through the crowded narrow streets toward temple hill.

There was a light in his eye and a joy in his aged step. A little over a month before, the shepherds had roused Jerusalem with the news of Messiah's birth at Bethlehem. At that time he knew it would not be long before he looked upon the One the centuries had waited for.

He knew he was going to have a prearranged meeting—but the place and the person he was going to meet were unknown to him. He searched the crowded temple area. The smell of burnt animal flesh hung heavy on the air. Priests and Levites mingled with northern peasants and Judean Pharisees. Bright blue robes rubbed rough sheepskin.

In the midst of the crowd he saw a couple holding a babe, moving from the court of women where purification would have been performed. They were obviously peasants unused to the crowds, din, and vastness of the temple. He knew that they were the reason he had been directed to the temple.

It was as if he had always known that this woman carried the Lord's Anointed. That baby was the focus of all the Law and the prophets. He stepped in front of the young couple and quietly took the babe from the mother's arms, saying:

> "Now Lord, Thou dost let Thy bond-
> servant depart
> In peace, according to Thy word;
> For my eyes have seen Thy salvation,
> Which Thou hast prepared in the pre-
> sence of all peoples,
> A LIGHT OF REVELATION TO THE GENTILES,
> And the glory of Thy people Israel."
> And His father and mother were amazed
> at the things which were being said about
> Him.

> Luke 2:28-33

Simeon saw a universal Messiah and Israel's glory not found in a bloody nationalism, but in this One he now worshiped. He then turned to the parents, blessed them, and solemnly said:

> "Behold, this Child is appointed for the
> fall and rise of many in Israel, and for a sign
> to be opposed—
> "and a sword will pierce even your own
> soul—to the end that thoughts from many
> hearts may be revealed."

> Luke 2:34-35

Hardly had he finished before Anna, the prophetess who never left the temple, came and joined the group. She began to give thanks to God and, turning to the rapidly growing crowd, spoke of the baby as being the redeemer of Israel.

Mary was silent on the return trip to Bethlehem, adding the latest announcements to all the other puzzling words hidden in her heart.

9

"The Kingdom Is at Hand"

The son of Zacharias and Elizabeth grew into manhood in the isolation of the Judean hills. His education was in the scrolls of the Law and the prophets. His classroom was the vastness of the Dead Sea wilderness, where rocks scorched the flesh on contact. He was dressed in a coat of camel skin; his diet was locusts and wild honey. He pored over the scrolls of the prophets and came to the villages with messages as blistering as the burning rocks where they had been born.

He was of the same order as all the prophets that had preceded him, stretching all the way back to Moses. But he was unique in his message. Every prophet had spoken of the king who was coming and the glorious kingdom He would set up. John spoke of the king as already being there, and the kingdom at hand. The hope of Israel was about to enter history, and John was His herald.

His message was a call to repent in the light of the imminent approach of the rule of Shiloh. The fierceness of his words and the content of his message drew crowds of peasants and fishermen from the Judean countryside and Galilee in the north. It wasn't long before the religious hierarchy from Jerusalem came to investigate and question John's credentials. Before many months the impact of his message would be felt as far away as Asia.

His message was simple and to the point: "The kingdom of heaven is at hand" (Matthew 3:2). The expression *kingdom of heaven* focused in one phrase all the hopes of the prophets. It was the kingdom promised to David, over which his descendant would reign forever. Within that kingdom was the blessing of Abraham, which his seed would bring to the world. It was the Zion of everlasting joy and unspeakable peace where the new covenant of forgiveness and righteousness would hold absolute sway. The expression centered in the Lord in human flesh, the virgin's child born, the Son given, the Wonderful Counselor, the Prince of Peace in whom Isaiah had long ago exulted. It was a kingdom not fashioned by human hands, but from God, that would reduce the kingdom of the world colossus to powder.

Proclaimed John: that kingdom is *now at hand!* The expression was a most urgent one. It indicated that the promised kingdom was about to burst upon the world at any moment, poised like a wave about to crash down upon the beach. In this phrase, *at hand,* he became a unique prophet, the only one to announce God's promises as about to be fulfilled in the immediate lifetime of his hearers.

John was an enigma to the fanatics of Judaism. He stood on the smooth boulders of Jordan and called the masses to repent. He proclaimed a Messiah who demanded righteousness, not swords. The preparation for the manifestation of the kingdom was not to carry arms but to repent, and to express repentance in ceremonial baptism in the Jordan River.

Religion was represented in the crowd, nervously fingering the tassels of their robes. The Pharisees and scribes made it abundantly clear that they considered themselves outside the challenge of John's message. They were the sons of Abraham and, in their opinion, the first subjects of Messiah's realm.

John was the voice of the remnant and called to the representatives of Israel to understand exactly who the true receivers of the promise were. It was not the blood descendants of Abraham, but those who exercised Abraham's faith.

> He therefore began saying to the multitudes who were going out to be baptized by him, "You brood of vipers, who warned you to flee from the wrath to come?
> Therefore bring forth fruits in keeping with your repentance, and do not begin to say to yourselves, 'We have Abraham for our father,' for I say to you that God is able from these stones to raise up children to Abraham."
>
> Luke 3:7-8

Their claim to the promises of God was a state of heart, not of descent and genealogical tables.

When John announced such a kingdom, he placed himself and the remnant, whose voice he was, in the absolute minority. Rome and its puppet, Herod, watched him closely, afraid that his inflammatory words would spark another suicidal revolution. On the other hand, young zealots who usually flocked to such a cause stood back, not wanting to be identified with John's concept of Messiah's kingdom. Religion normally played its cards between the two, but John had publicly stripped the phony religious leaders, and now they bitterly licked their wounds, vowing revenge.

But if there was no violence and call to arms, how could the kingdom of Messiah become a reality? What would Messiah do to bring about the fulfillment of the glorious prophecies?

John did not merely call the people *from* sin and national pride, but *to* the utterly different kingdom of Messiah. That kingdom was to be known in a vital union with the Holy Spirit: "I baptized you with water; but He will baptize you with the Holy Spirit" (Mark 1:8).

his proclamation of John's was the first ray of light that, within the next four years, was to become the blazing light of a new day in which all the words of the prophets would be understood. The words and promises of the prophets could come to pass only in a vital relationship to the Holy Spirit. He paralleled this relationship to the baptism he gave his converts in Jordan.

Messiah was going to bring His subjects into the same relationship with the Spirit that the converts of John had to the waters of Jordan. The Messiah was going to plunge men into the Spirit so that the

Spirit would be the element in which they moved and a vital power and source of life within them.

The audience on the banks of Jordan re-membered the words of the prophet: "And I will put My Spirit within you and cause you to walk in My statutes" (Ezekiel 36:27).

John left the current ideas of Messiah's person and work in pieces. He drew his listeners back to the true message of the prophets and then carried them on to fulfillment in the kingdom that Messiah would bring about in giving the Spirit.

Israel, the physical nation, a kingdom of earth among other nations; with its city of Jerusalem; with its the earthly throne of David; with its kings, its borders, and the temple with its priesthood and sacrifices—all had been a shadow of the true substance. Now the shadow had to yield to it. Israel's future glory was not in her earthly continuance, but in her relationship to the Spirit through the Messiah.

If Israel rejected this, seeking an earthly kingdom, continuing on a path of covenant breaking, it would find itself under the ax of judgment:

> And also the axe is already laid at the root of the trees; every tree therefore that does not bear good fruit is cut down and thrown into the fire. . . .
> And His winnowing fork is in His hand to clean out His threshing floor, and to gather the wheat into His barn; but He will burn up the chaff with unquenchable fire.
> Luke 3:9, 17

The kingdom of Messiah could not be seen, understood, or entered into except through submission to Messiah and an experiential union with the Holy Spirit. Only in the Holy Spirit could the words of the prophets actually take place.

It was at this time that Jesus came from Galilee to the banks of the Jordan river, joining the milling crowds gathered to John. Born of the Holy Spirit, God in human nature, He had, for thirty years, developed normally, facing all of life as a true man. He had faced and resisted the real temptations of a growing teenager and a young man.

He had worked with His father, Joseph, and faced the responsibility of being the eldest in a large family. Now the time had come for Him to be publicly announced as the Messiah. John had already announced Him as the One whose shoes he was not worthy to unloose. Now that One stood unknown and unnoticed in the crowd, the carpenter from Nazareth. The crowds jostled Him on either side. John suddenly declared, "I baptize in water, but among you stands One whom you do not know. It is He who comes after me, the thong of whose sandal I am not worthy to untie" (John 1:26-27).

The next day, as the crowd dispersed, a knot of disciples stood around John. Jesus walked through the thinning crowd. John pointed to Him and in hushed tones announced, "Behold, the Lamb of God who takes away the sin of the world! This is He on behalf of whom I said, 'After me comes a Man who has a higher rank than I, for He existed before me'" (John 1:29-30).

When Jesus stepped out of the crowd and presented Himself to John for baptism, John was aghast. He had repeatedly said that he was not worthy to be Messiah's most lowly slave. Now the One who was so glorious, to whom being His slave would have been man's highest dignity, had asked for baptism. Certainly Jesus was not repenting in asking for baptism, for He had nothing to repent of. In this act, He was identifying Himself with the remnant, the true Israel.

It was a decision made before time, that had actualized in the virgin birth, now proclaimed before the watching multitude. In this act, He officially embarked upon the decision eternally made, for which He had been born.

Isaiah had called Messiah the servant of the Lord, who would live a life of perfect servitude to God the Father, obeying Him even unto death. What Jesus now stated in baptism had been the set of His will since His earliest years. As He had grown in maturity as a man, so this attitude had grown with Him. His earliest understanding was demonstrated in a brief record of His life at the age of twelve.

From birth through the age of twelve, a Jewish boy was educated in the Law of Moses. At the age of twelve, education was over and he would go to Jerusalem, where, after oral examination by the rabbis, he would be accepted as a full member of the congregation of Israel, a son of the Law—*Bar Mitzvah*. After this he would begin to learn his father's trade, taking his place as a man in Israel.

Jesus was no exception. He was a true man, and went through all that the Law of Israel demanded. At twelve years of age, after having learned and practiced the Law of Moses, He was taken to the temple in Jerusalem for Bar Mitzvah. After

101

this, He would return to Nazareth to be apprenticed to His father in the art of carpentry.

Having been accepted as a son of the Law, He would normally have returned to His father's shop for apprenticeship. He gently pointed out to His earthly parents that Joseph was not His father by indicating to them that He must now begin an apprenticeship to His true Father and the work for which He was born. His first act of submission to His true Father, however, was to be submissive to His earthly father, His guardian through life.

Throughout His teenage years, He learned obedience to His heavenly Father and in so doing, grew into the maturity of servanthood for which Israel as a nation had always been intended. This was not a charade. Although He was God, He had laid aside all the prerogatives and powers of deity and faced life as true man in the power of the Holy Spirit.

His teenage years were described by those who knew Him: "And Jesus kept increasing in wisdom and stature, and in favor with God and men" (Luke 2:52).

The expression, *increasing,* means to cut a way through, as a pioneer. Jesus lived and made decisions that no other teenager ever had. He hacked a way through the jungle of selfishness and sin, amidst a people who lived in the lie. He made decisions and choices based on light and truth, the first of His kind. Isaiah had described this learning process centuries before:

> The Lord God has given Me the tongue
> of disciples,
> That I may know how to sustain the
> weary one with a word.
> He awakens Me morning by morning,

He awakens My ear to listen as a dis-
ciple.
The Lord God has opened My ear;
And I was not disobedient,
Nor did I turn back.

Isaiah 50:4-5

Now after the years of costly, sinless choices, He
presented Himself for baptism. It was a public
declaration of who He was. For all who stepped into the
Jordan, the act was a *change* of mind. But He was
expressing a *state* of mind that had always been His.

Isaiah had spoken much of the servant of the Lord
when describing Messiah. He had seen Him as the
beloved and precious of the Lord. As Jesus came out of
the Jordan after baptism, a voice filled the desert air:
"This is My beloved Son, in whom I am well-pleased"
(Matthew 3:17). It was an echo of the prophet and the
testimony of God to the character and person of the
servant of the Lord.

The testimony was culminated in the Holy Spirit
coming upon Him. To the watching John, the Spirit
appeared as a descending dove. It was for such a sign
that John had been waiting. He shared with his disciples:

"I have beheld the Spirit descending as
a dove out of heaven; and He remained upon
Him.
"And I did not recognize Him, but He
who sent me to baptize in water said to me,
'He upon whom you see the Spirit descending and remaining upon Him, this is the
one who baptizes in the Holy Spirit.'
"And I have seen, and have borne
witness that this is the Son of God."

John 1:32-34

103

He was the Messiah, the Christ, the Anointed One from birth, for as such He had been announced to the shepherds. This was the public anointing marking His entrance to the work for which He had been born. It was an assurance from the Father to His servant that He truly was the Messiah, as well as to the remnant who had eagerly awaited Him. It was the throwing down of the gauntlet in the dark world where Satan ruled as the pretend prince. The deliverer of God's creation was publicly announced.

As Jesus stood in the Jordan River, He was endued with the Spirit from on high. In the power of the Spirit, He would carry man into the holiest of all, the true Zion. Prophet, priest, and king found their final substance and reality in Him who walked up the slippery bank of the river and into the wilderness—with the Holy Spirit upon Him.

10

Thieves in the Temple

The ornate temple that dominated Jerusalem was Israel's true center. Within its precincts was her national charter. Their existence as a nation was based on the fact that the Lord was their God and they were His people. That awesome relationship was worked out within the temple, and so it was that the eyes of every Israelite turned to those courts as the heart of his religion and his citizenship.

The labyrinth of passages, the vast courts, the multitudes of chambers and porches were all filled with white-robed priests, the sons of Levi, who had represented the nation before God since Aaron. They offered the never-ending sacrifices that had been given by God to hallow His name and grant the people the right to call Him "their God," and themselves "His people." The air of the temple was constantly impregnated with the smell of roasting flesh as the curling blue smoke ascended from the altar of burnt offering—a reminder of the relationship between God and the people.

But Israel had come a long way from Aaron, the first high priest. Sounds that were never known in Solomon's temple came from within the sacred walls. Annas and his son-in-law, Caiaphas, held the office of high priest and directed the religious life of both the nation within the land of Israel and the scattered nation throughout the Roman empire. His control was not that of a spiritual father, but more that of a godfather of organized crime.

The most infamous and lucrative of all his activities was known as the Bazaar of the sons of Annas. It was a large section of the temple in which Annas conducted a business of extortion that filled his coffers with gold.

Passover was the time when profits ran high. A month before, every town in Israel would know the arrival of the money changer. He set up his table to receive the temple tax, the half-shekel payable to the temple by every Israelite male. It was not as simple as that, however. The tax had to be paid in sacred coinage—temple money. Israel used a multitude of coinage because of its being the Roman highway between the north and Egypt and Africa. The rate of exchange was high in favor of the money changers. This went on for ten days. After that, the changers went into the Bazaar of the sons of Annas in the temple at Jerusalem to prepare for the hundreds of thousands of pilgrims coming from the far corners of the Roman world.

Pilgrims came to change more than half-shekels for temple tax. They brought bags of cash to turn into sacred coin in order to buy animals for sacrifice and give their money offerings. An offerer could bring his own animal sacrifice with him, but it was easier to buy on the temple premises. If an animal was brought for sacrifice that had not been purchased at the temple, it had to be examined, at further cost in sacred coin, and most of the time would be rejected as unfit for sacrifice.

The Bazaar sold for sacrifice the animals that had already been declared as fit. The sons of Annas made sure the prices made their trouble worthwhile. The dove, or pigeon—offerings allowed for the very poor—cost a Roman gold coin and half again after it had been changed to temple coinage.

The covenant relationship was broken. The temple was a mocking reminder of what once had been and was now a hollow memory. In the name of God's holiness, man was reaping corrupt mammon. The courts, where the blood sacrifice vindicated God's holiness until Messiah came, were now putrid with greed. Man had taken God's gift of salvation and prostituted it for gain.

Into the Bazaar of the sons of Annas came Jesus, Son of the holy One. He surveyed the scene. The stench of animal refuse filled the air. Above the noise of the bleating of sheep and lowing of cattle were the curses and arguments of money changers defending their extortion, and angry worshipers who knew they were being cheated in the name of the Lord. The scene was that of a hall of racketeers. Anyone who came here to worship the covenant God, after losing money in the exchanges and buying a sacrifice for twice its real value, would forget why he came in the first place.

When a rabbi lifted his sash above his head in anger, it was a symbol of his condemnation of all around him. Jesus was a peasant from Galilee, and His sash was a rope tied around His tunic. He undid it and raised it above His head in holy anger. The people fell back, excited. They had long awaited someone who would proclaim justice and beat the servants of Annas.

Jesus moved through the parting crowd. A table of a money changer was in front of Him. With His free hand, He lifted it and sent the coins flying in all directions. Another followed and another. Money changers fought on the floor, grappling for the money that flew in all directions. He opened the pens of the animals, sheep and oxen stampeded across the Bazaar.

Men cursed, animals fled, the birds filled the air. In the middle stood the teacher from Galilee, His rope sash in hand above His head, an awful personalizing of God's wrath on Israel in broken covenant. The official priests, serfs of Annas, came running, holding their robes around them. They licked their lips nervously.

The mood of the large crowd was obvious; they watched with glee, ready to tear, limb from limb, anyone who laid a hand on Jesus. His voice echoed, distinct and clear for all to hear, "Take these things away; stop making My Father's house a house of merchandise" (John 2:16).

The authorities responded weakly, asking for a sign to prove His authority. They didn't need a sign, for their conscience had long told them of their wrong, but they pressed the point to save face. He responded, "Destroy this temple, and in three days I will raise it up" (John 2:19). There was a silence that quieted even the excitement in the crowd. *Destroy the temple? Build another? In three days?* The ideas were unheard of.

To destroy the temple would be to destroy Israel's heart. The whole system of approach to God, the priesthood, the offerings—*destroyed?* All that they had learned from the Law of Moses, for which they were willing to die, destroyed by this madman?

Replace it with another that He would personally build in three days? The glorious religion of Moses would never be replaced. One of the priests, a smile flickering on his lips, said, "It took forty-six years to build this temple, and will You raise it up in three days?" (John 2:20).

The crowd began to disperse. Everyone pondered His words of revolution.

The temple was the subject of another dis-cussion within the week. Jesus and the group of disciples that had gathered around Him journeyed north to Capernaum in Galilee, their hometown. Starting out at the chill dawn, they had walked into Samaria by noon. The Jews hated the Samaritans, avoiding their section of the country by crossing the Jordan to skirt it. Jesus had insisted on going right through it.

By noon, Jesus and all of the disciples were hungry and thirsty. They had made it to Jacob's Well in Sychar and decided to stop there for lunch. Jesus and the youngest disciple sat in the shade of the well's shelter while the others went into the nearby town for food.

Through the shimmering heat haze, a woman with a water pot on her shoulder approached them. She came to where they were sitting, and Jesus asked her for a drink. Her response was brittle with the hatred between the two peoples: "How is it that You, being a Jew, ask me for a drink since I am a Samaritan woman?" (John 4:9). Jesus was unruffled, offering her the gift He had come to give the race: "If you knew the gift of God, and who it is who says to you, 'Give Me a drink,' you would have asked Him, and He would have given you living water" (John 4:10).

She wanted the water of life of which he spoke, but had no desire to face up to the emptiness and tragedy that her selfishness had produced. She quickly changed the subject. It was obvious she was in dialogue with a man of God and so threw out a question that always promised a lively religious debate among Jews and Samaritans: "Sir, I perceive that You are a prophet. Our fathers worshiped in this mountain; and you people say that in Jerusalem is the place where men ought to worship" (John 4:19-20).

The answer of Jesus was quite unexpected:

> "Woman, believe Me, an hour is coming when neither in this mountain, nor in Jerusalem, shall you worship the Father.
>
> "You worship that which you do not know; we worship that which we know; for salvation is from the Jews.
>
> "But an hour is coming, and now is, when the true worshipers shall worship the Father in spirit and truth; for such people the Father seeks to be His worshipers.

"God is spirit; and those who worship
Him must worship in spirit and truth."
John 4:21-24

It was a restatement of what He had said to the
Jewish leaders. At the present time, the temple, with its
Levitical system of priests and sacrifices, was right and
the expression of God's covenant. Salvation was
contained among the Jews. But a new day was coming
when what was now right, if continued in, would be
wrong. That day was both coming and, in a sense,
already at hand, when Jerusalem and the temple would
no longer be the focus of worship. In that day already
dawning, worship would not be found in a company
gathering in the temple, but in a company gathered in
the Spirit, a union with God who is Spirit. The location
of worship would no more be bricks and mortar, but in
the dimension of the Spirit. *The dimension of Spirit was
going to constitute a new kind of temple.*

The glorious kingdom under Messiah was called
Zion, a company of people in such relationship to
God as to live in the holiest of all. Jesus now
revealed *how* that was to be built. *The new temple,
Zion, the subject of the ancient prophets, was to be
found not in Jerusalem, but in the Spirit.*

All the shadows of reality found in the temple
and the tabernacle, and Mount Zion before it, would
find their substance in Messiah's temple in the
Spirit. The destroying of the temple, the new day
of the temple to be built in three days, was not a
new religion, but Judaism come of age.

The woman vaguely knew her Scriptures and
recognized the content of what He was saying as having
to do with the age of Messiah of the last days. She
shrugged, trying to terminate the conversation. "I know

111

that Messiah is coming (He who is called Christ); when that One comes, He will declare all things to us" (John 4:25).

Jesus said to her, "I who speak to you am He" (John 4:26.)

The hope of Israel had declared Himself.

11

A Teacher Learns

Caiaphas, the high priest, chairman of the Great Sanhedrin, the supreme court of Israel, and son-in-law of Annas, fumed at the words of Jesus in the temple. No one called Caiaphas a viper as John the Baptist previously had, or his family a den of thieves, and got away with it. Certainly not some itinerant preacher from the peasants of Galilee.

It was not only Caiaphas who felt that way. The entire council of the Sanhedrin was incensed by the recent events. The Great Sanhedrin over which the high priest presided was made up of seventy men. They were the most religious men and the brilliant brains of the nation. By conviction they fell into two categories: *Sadducee and Pharisee.*

The *Sadducee* party, for the most part rich and conservative, accepted only the written Law of Moses and were lax in keeping it. The family of Annas, constituting the priestly section of that august body, were Sadducees, as were some of the elders. The elders, or the ancients, were laymen who had been elected to the Sanhedrin because of the reputation they gained over the years, and who were respected locally for their wisdom.

Other elders—along with the young doctors and lawyers, called *scribes*—were *Pharisees*. The Pharisees accepted not only the written Law of Moses, but also the oral tradition handed down by generations of rabbis. These traditions filled volumes, and the Pharisees obeyed them all with great devotion and show of piety. Across the country the common laborers looked upon the Pharisees as holy men, listening to them and obeying them even when they openly contradicted the Sadducean high priest.

John had called these leaders—the most respected Pharisees—a generation of snakes. He accused them of being full of poison under their guise of religion. They had been stung to rage. Then Jesus had called the Bazaar of Annas the Sadducee a den of thieves. The seventy bearded wise men of Israel could finally agree on one issue as they sat in semicircle in the chamber of hewn stones within the temple precincts: John and Jesus must be silenced. Their statements could quickly inflame the peasants to revolt and cause trouble with Rome.

The current Sanhedrin council was weak, for Caiaphas was a strong high priest and the seventy were willing to simply follow him. The weakness of the court made Caiaphas the most powerful man in Judea, as Herod was in Galilee. Both were puppets under Roman rule but enjoyed great power. Caiaphas had absolute power in religious matters, and a large say in civil affairs. It was a foolhardy man who fell out with the family of Annas, worse still to add to that the anger of the Pharisee party.

But within the body were some who had more in mind than keeping peace with Rome. They talked of the coming kingdom, the ancient prophecies, and Messiah. One of this quiet minority was Nicodemus. He and those with whom he shared his innermost longings regarded John with interest and Jesus with subdued admiration.

Nicodemus was one of the elders; in fact, he was the most respected ancient on the council and was referred to as *the* teacher in Israel. The old Pharisee was not about to brush Jesus aside for His action in the temple. It was a rather hasty action, but long overdue. He had listened to what Jesus had to say as He spoke in the temple porches, and watched His miracles. There was something about the Galilean's words that set the old man's heart on fire. He decided to speak with Jesus for himself. To speak with Jesus in a serious dialogue could cause him the loss of his credibility. For a man of his standing to have a theological discussion with a peasant from Galilee was socially unacceptable.

So the old Pharisee came by night to talk with Jesus. He began cautiously summing up the feelings of the minority he unofficially represented: "Rabbi, we know that You have come from God as a teacher; for no one can do these signs that You do unless God is with him" (John 3:2).

Jesus did not answer his remark. He looked beyond his words to what Nicodemus was saying within himself and spoke to all his pent-up cries and longings for God's kingdom to come. In the Galilean's answer, all the masks Nicodemus had ever worn were thrown aside, and the respected teacher became a pupil. Jesus said to him, "Truly, truly, I say to you, unless one is born again, he cannot see the kingdom of God" (John 3:3).

The gentle words passed judgment on all Nicodemus had ever considered himself as being. His national and religious pride rose within him. *Was he not a son of Abraham, a Pharisee, keeper of the Law and of the traditions of the rabbis? If anyone was ready for entrance into the kingdom, was it not a pious man like himself? Was this young man telling him he must begin a new life?*

What Jesus was calling for had nothing to do with human genealogy, even if it began with Abraham. *That* had been given Nicodemus by his parents. The life Jesus spoke of had to be given by God. God's kingdom is not a matter of physical descent, or national blood. *Jesus was saying that no one could be born physically into God's kingdom.* The only entrance into this kingdom was to be born spiritually of the Spirit; in fact, it could only be *seen* by being born of the Spirit. All the subjects of Messiah's kingdom were to be Spirit-born.

As the spring wind blew and tugged at nearby trees there was a gentle sound of rustling leaves. Jesus remarked, "The wind blows where it wishes and you hear the sound of it, but do not know where it comes from and where it is going; so is every one who is born of the Spirit" (John 3:8). Nicodemus looked bewildered, asking, "How can these things be?" (John 3:9).

Compassion filled the eyes of the young man looking at the furrows of question above the bushy gray brows. He leaned forward with genuine inquiry. "Are you the teacher of Israel, and do not understand these things?" (John 3:10). To Jesus it was almost incredible. Were these men so wrapped up in their national hopes and ideas of a kingdom that they had not heard what the Scriptures had said? The prophets had said that the kingdom was made up of the blood-washed and Spirit-born. In fact all that Jesus had said that night was almost a quotation from the prophet Ezekiel.

When Israel had been carried in chains to Babylon centuries before, the young Ezekiel had encouraged the captives by showing them that the purposes of God reached beyond the immediate history. A glorious kingdom would yet be established and ruled over by Messiah.

The return to the land was important—but not as important as what would happen after they returned to their possessions. At that time they would receive an inward cleansing from guilt and defilement. It would be accompanied by a coming within them of the Spirit that would cause them to walk spontaneously in the Law of the Lord:

> Then I will sprinkle clean water on you, and you will be clean; I will cleanse you from all your filthiness and from all your idols.
>
> Moreover, I will give you a new heart and put a new spirit within you; and I will remove the heart of stone from your flesh and give you a heart of flesh.

117

> And I will put My Spirit within you and
> cause you to walk in My statutes, and you
> will be careful to observe My ordinances.
>
> Ezekiel 36:25-27

In order to have a clearer picture of this, Ezekiel was taken in a vision to a valley of death. From end to end the valley was filled with dry, bleached bones—the remains of a great army.

The Spirit urged Ezekiel to take a tour of the valley and investigate the situation. The bones were very dry, brittle with age. Then came a question from God: "Can these bones live?" (Ezekiel 37:3).

The question sounded like utter foolishness. The situation was hopeless, not even within the realm of reason. But Ezekiel had been around the Lord long enough to put the question back to Him: "O Lord God, Thou knowest" (Ezekiel 37:3).

Again the voice of God spoke, this time ordering him to preach to the bones. As he did so there was a great noise as every bone in the valley came together with its fellow bone, making skeletons that momentarily covered the floor of the chasm. This was followed by sinews, muscle, and flesh. The valley had advanced from a bone yard to a mortuary. The Lord commanded again, "Prophesy to the breath, prophesy, son of man, and say to the breath, 'Thus says the Lord God, "Come from the four winds, O breath, and breathe on these slain, that they come to life" '" (Ezekiel 37:9). In the Hebrew language the word for *breath* is also the word for *spirit or wind*.

Ezekiel did as he was commanded and the wind rushed through the valley. But it was more than wind, it was the creative breath of God; for at its touch the army came alive, resurrected with the life of the Spirit within them. This was life that they had never had before. It was life from the dead. An army of dead-alive ones. A resurrected people.

This was the miracle that God was going to work in His people after they had returned to their land. *They would be Israel, but in another form—a resurrected Israel alive with the life of the Spirit.*

The long captivity came to an end and, as all the prophets had said. They returned and settled again in their land, led by Ezra and Nehemiah. But the prophecies all spoke of the miracle of Messiah's kingdom *after that.* So they waited for a washing of water within, a birthing of the Spirit that they might be the great army of reborn ones.

The kingdom of Messiah is inhabited by those who have seen that they are dead toward God; that their spiritual condition is as dry and empty of true life as the bones of death valley were in the natural sphere. For such there is no hope of seeing the kingdom, let alone entering it, until there is a rebirth, an enlivening with the life of the Spirit. Only after being reborn can anyone see the kingdom that, as John had previously pointed out, was in the realm of the Spirit.

Nicodemus went away puzzled but with a longing rising within him. He could not shrug off the man from Galilee. The wind tugged at his blue robe, and he remembered, ". . . so is every one who is born of the Spirit" (John 3:8). The wind of God would blow on the valley of death, and Messiah's kingdom would *be.*

12

Healing for the Whole Man

John the Baptist had been thrown into jail by King Herod. His crime was that he had publicly called upon Herod to repent of his many sins. Now he languished in a dungeon under Herod's castle in the area of the Dead Sea. He wondered whether he had been mistaken. Was it not time he received news of Jesus announcing Himself as king of the world? All he heard from his visiting disciples was of crowds flocking to hear teachings of love and to behold miracle cures. Is *that* the kingdom? Is Jesus really Messiah? The presence of Rome and the court of Herod mocked John in his doubts in his dark cell.

The dismal dungeon and the constant presence of the power of evil in Herod's men caused his gnawing doubts. To his visiting disciples he voiced his despair and sent them with a typically blunt question to Jesus:

"John the Baptist has sent us to You, saying, 'Are You the One who is coming, or do we look for someone else?'"

At that very time He cured many people of diseases and afflictions and evil spirits; and He granted sight to many who were blind.

And He answered and said to them, "Go and report to John what you have seen and heard: the BLIND RECEIVE SIGHT, the lame walk, the lepers are cleansed, and the deaf hear, the dead are raised up, the POOR HAVE THE GOSPEL PREACHED TO THEM.

And blessed is he who keeps from stumbling over Me."

Luke 7:20-23

Jesus reminded John in His reply that the Law and the prophets had spoken of people being healed and leaping and shouting with joy:

Then the eyes of the blind will be opened,
And the ears of the deaf will be unstopped.
Then the lame will leap like a deer,
And the tongue of the dumb will shout for joy

Isaiah 35:5-6

The love power that would ultimately revolutionize the heavens and the earth was now being released.

John was not the only puzzled questioner. The zealots, a group of fanatical Jews intent on bringing about Messiah's kingdom by force, watched Jesus with curiosity. He spoke words of love and used His power only for love ends, blessing all He came in contact with. Why didn't He use His awesome power to destroy the Roman militia? Power that could still a storm with a word, turn water into wine, and heal all diseases could certainly disintegrate a Roman garrison.

Jesus *had* declared war on the enemy, but not against Rome or any other human power. He was at war against the forces that held human beings captive since the fall—Satan and his demons. It was a force that held the entire person captive.

The earliest prophecies describing the mission of Messiah had been of His delivering man from the bondage of Satan and restoring him to fellowship with God. This deliverance was not only in the realm of the spirit and soul but also of the body. The Hebrews never thought of a person as a dichotomy of spirit and body, but as one whole person. To speak of God's salvation being for man, it was understood to be for the whole man. Believing the lie, surrendering to the liar, had affected the whole person; and salvation would have to be for that whole person to be salvation at all.

Into a wretched darkness had come Messiah Jesus announcing the regenerating of man in the kingdom to be in the Spirit. From the pulpit of His hometown synagogue He had declared war on the true enemies of man. He had entered the syna-gogue on the Sabbath and was given the scroll of the Prophet Isaiah to read:

> And He opened the book, and found the
> place where it was written,
>> "THE SPIRIT OF THE LORD IS UPON ME,
>> BECAUSE HE ANOINTED ME TO PREACH THE
>> GOSPEL TO THE POOR.
>> HE HAS SENT ME TO PROCLAIM RELEASE TO
>> THE CAPTIVES,
>> AND RECOVERY OF SIGHT TO THE BLIND,
>> TO SET FREE THOSE WHO ARE DOWN-
>> TRODDEN,
>> TO PROCLAIM THE FAVORABLE YEAR OF THE
>> LORD."
>
> Luke 4:18-19

The Prophet Isaiah was taking one of the ancient customs of the Jews and seeing in it a prophetical forecast of the future reign of Messiah. The custom he referred to was the Year of Jubilee, which occurred every fiftieth year. The main thrust of Jubilee was restoration of the nation to normality. All who had lost lands because of poverty or debts had them returned. Slaves working off bad debts or those in debtor's prison were released to a fresh start. It was a time of hilarious joy accompanied by a year of holy vacation to God's glory. The prophet had seen the day of Messiah as the fulfillment of every concept of Jubilee. From the wretched misery and slavery of guilt and darkness, the Messiah would restore humanity to normality.

Jesus finished His reading in the synagogue with the explosive words "Today this Scripture had been fulfilled in your hearing" (Luke 4:21).

This was the kingdom He had come to establish, as surely as the war He had come to be victor in. All the sick, distorted, elements in human beings were to be transformed, renewed, healed, so that the life of God could be fully expressed through them. Jesus had gone through Galilee and Judea healing the sick, casting out demons, restoring humanity to normality:

> And Jesus was going about in all Galilee, teaching in their synagogues, and proclaiming the gospel of the kingdom, and healing every kind of disease and every kind of sickness among the people.
>
> And the news about Him went out into all Syria; and they brought to Him all who were ill, taken with various diseases and pains, demoniacs, epileptics, paralytics; and He healed them.
>
> And great multitudes followed Him from Galilee and Decapolis and Jerusalem and Judea and from beyond the Jordan.
>
> Matthew 4:23-25

> And when evening had come, they brought to Him many who were demon-possessed; and He cast out the spirits with a word, and healed all who were ill.
>
> Matthew 8:16

> And when they had crossed over they came to land at Gennesaret, and moored to the shore.
>
> And when they had come out of the boat, immediately the people recognized Him,
>
> and ran about that whole country and began to carry about on their pallets those who were sick, to the place they heard He was.

> And wherever He entered villages, or
> cities, or countryside, they were laying the
> sick in the market places, and entreating Him
> that they might just touch the fringe of His
> cloak; and as many as touched it were being
> cured.
>
> Mark 6:53-56

Isaiah had seen the descendant of Jesse as energized by the Spirit to fulfill His task: "And the Spirit of the Lord will rest on Him, The spirit of wisdom and understanding, The spirit of council and strength, The spirit of knowledge and the fear of the Lord" (Isaiah 11:2). With truth, wisdom, and understanding He would counsel the sick minds and emotions—and with strength, might, and power, He would bring healing to the sick bodies.

He called His miracles, *works*, which placed them in the category of the normal marks of the kingdom being present among men. On one occasion He said simply, "But if I cast out demons by the Spirit of God, then the kingdom of God has come upon you" (Matthew 12:28).

Jesus gathered around Him *disciples*—apprentices to Him—to prepare them to carry the news of the kingdom to the world. He sent them out on missions and showed them that to proclaim the arrival of the kingdom was to bring healing to the body. The healing of the sick was the medium through which the healing of man's spirit was announced:

> And He called the twelve together, and
> gave them power and authority over all the
> demons, and to heal diseases.

126

> And He sent them out to proclaim the
> kingdom of God, and to perform healing.
>
> Luke 9:1-2

Sin and sickness were seen to be the result of the Fall, and as such were dealt with in one blow by the deliverer, who was bringing about trans-formation to the whole man.

On one occasion a paralytic was lowered before Jesus for healing:

> "Take courage, My son [said Jesus], your sins are forgiven."
> And behold, some of the scribes said to themselves, "This fellow blasphemes."
> And Jesus knowing their thoughts said, "Why are you thinking evil in your hearts?
> For which is easier, to say, 'Your sins are forgiven,' or to say, 'Rise, and walk'?
> But in order that you may know that the Son of Man has authority on earth to forgive sins"—then He said to the paralytic, "Rise, take up your bed, and go home."
> And he rose, and went to his home.
> But when the multitudes saw this, they were filled with awe, and glorified God, who had given such authority to men.
>
> Matthew 9:2-8

By His words Jesus explained that His kingdom dealt equally with the spirit and the body.

The kingdom was not a philosophy of words but the actual entrance of the living God into the situation of wretched humanity, restoring it to wholeness. It was a kingdom in which transformation by new birth and the healing of the physical body by the same Spirit were brought to everyone who would believe in Jesus Messiah.

13

Righteousness and the Law

The Messiah had come, but few realized it. All they knew was that one walked among them who devastated all their cherished ideas.

It was with the Pharisees that Jesus had His worst clashes. It was inevitable, for they used the same words while speaking of different things. Both He and they were consumed with a passion for what they called righteousness—but their definitions for it were worlds apart.

Jesus came, the fulfillment of the Law of Moses, the Ten Commandments, the moral law as well as the ceremonial law. He was its most perfect expositor and its most perfect demonstrator. The Pharisees claimed to be just that, but alongside Jesus their piety was seen as shallow and tawdry. They were stung to fury by the exposure.

Their trouble was they had deified the Law to the point where the Law was seen as an entity in itself, something apart from God. They did not see

God as the Absolute from whom all law found its authority and in whom it found its meaning. He is the cohesion of the Ten Commandments, without whom there is no sense to Law. They had separated God from His Law and were left with meaningless and unrelated commands. Obedience to the Ten Commandments is of value only as it is done from the heart unto God for His glory.

The Pharisees were left keeping commands for the commands' sake and for their own protection. God, to them, was distant, angry, ready to punish all violations of His Law. To keep the Law was their protection against the wrath of God. To avoid transgression was to avoid punishment. The idea of God being in His commands—and the keeping of those commands for His sake being the end of all moral existence—was foreign to them.

Their emphasis was not on the positive keeping of commands *for His glory, but* rather on how to avoid breaking them *to protect themselves.* Determining in myriad ways how they may be broken became every Pharisee's obsession. Not seeing God in His commands, they ingeniously managed to avoid seeing what the commands actually said, while seeking to keep them in their outward form. In carrying out this outward form they became proficient in outdoing one another in religious competition.

To the Pharisee, righteousness was a matter of keeping the external form of the Law, and they worked at so doing night and day. Whenever outward conduct is emphasized more than inward, and wherever that outward conduct is equated with morality, the sins of self-righteousness and hypocrisy run rampant. The kingdom of Messiah was ever seen as one of righteousness, and Jesus came proclaiming it. Isaiah had seen the multitudes coming to Zion eager to be taught in the Law by Messiah the king. Further in his prophecy he had given a description of the king:

> But with righteousness He will judge the poor,
> And decide with fairness for the afflicted of the earth;
> And He will strike the earth with the rod of His mouth,
> And with the breath of His lips He will slay the wicked.
> Also righteousness will be the belt about His loins,
> And faithfulness the belt about His waist.
>
> Isaiah 11:4-5

Jeremiah had seen the age of Messiah as the writing of the Law on the hearts of people so that it became the principle of their actions from within.

When Jesus proclaimed such a kingdom of righteousness, He not only contradicted the Pharisees but also stung them to fury. To Him the Law was the expression among men of God's holiness, and therefore not to be rationalized in outward forms, but in it to be confronted by God. He was the all-seeing One to whom actions meant nothing unless they came from the source of a worshiping heart.

The Pharisees' outward actions made a show of piety, but before the all-seeing eye of God, they were full of corruption. To His disciples, Jesus insisted that their righteousness had to go beyond the definition that Pharisaism had given to the word: "For I say to you, that unless your righteousness surpasses that of the scribes and Pharisees, you shall not enter the kingdom of heaven" (Matthew 5:20). This was a shock to the peasants who heard Him. To them the Pharisee was the holy man, the model of any righteousness they ever hoped to attain to. The shuffling Pharisee praying his long prayer on a street corner was the foretaste of Messiah's kingdom. The idea of a righteousness that was within the heart, lodged in the thoughts and delight of the one who practiced it, was as old as Moses, but new to the Israel of their day.

Jesus described His disciples, the subjects of Messiah's kingdom, as a company who hungered and thirsted after righteousness (Matthew 5:6). To these, righteousness was life itself, and they would rather suffer than turn from it (Matthew 5:10).

When Jesus taught, He equated the kingdom with righteousness (Matthew 6:33). The kingdom was never seen as a physical structure, or the bringing in of a political order, but always as the doing of God's will. He taught them this was to be their first petition when praying (Matthew 6:10).

The Pharisees had expanded the Law to thousands of directions and regulations, all the time moving away from its true meaning. Jesus reduced the Law to a few words and came directly to the spirit of it:

> One . . . asked Him . . . "Teacher, which
> is the great commandment in the Law?"
> And He said to him, " 'YOU SHALL LOVE
> THE LORD YOUR GOD WITH ALL YOUR HEART,
> AND WITH ALL YOUR SOUL, AND WITH ALL YOUR
> MIND.'
> "This is the great and foremost com-
> mandment. And a second is like it, 'YOU
> SHALL LOVE YOUR NEIGHBOR AS YOURSELF.'
> "On these two commandments depend
> the whole Law and the Prophets."
> Matthew 22:36-40

Actions spring from within, therefore it is within that man had to be righteous if the actions were to be worth anything. The subjects of the kingdom were seen to be righteous—reproducers, expressers of the nature and will of God, revelators of His light. Jesus said:

> "You are the light of the world. A city
> set on a hill cannot be hidden.
> "Nor do men light a lamp, and put it
> under the peck-measure, but on the lamp-
> stand; and it gives light to all who are in the
> house.
> "Let your light shine before men in such
> a way that they may see your good works,
> and glorify your Father who is in heaven."
> Matthew 5:14-16

But how could this be? How could any live in the kingdom if the subjects were so righteous as to be acceptable to God's infinite holy gaze? The

Good News that Jesus came with was that man could never achieve that of himself. The righteousness that was found in His kingdom was given by God. Only God's righteousness could satisfy God's holiness.

The first step into the kingdom was to admit that all had to be received *from* God. "Blessed are *the poor in spirit,* for theirs is the kingdom of heaven" (Matthew 5:3, author's italics). Only those who were helpless enough to receive from God could hope for such righteousness. All man could do was summed up in hungering and thirsting; God had to give His righteousness: "Blessed are those who hunger and thirst for righteousness, for they shall be satisfied" (Matthew 5:6).

The Pharisees despised all who did not fashion their behavior and lifestyle according to their pietistic rules. First on their list of despicable characters were the tax gatherers. These were renegade Jews who had sold out to the Romans and now collected taxes from their countrymen for Rome. Along with the taxes they collected an excess that found its way into their own coffers.

Jesus made such men His special friends and spoke to them of a God different from the God of the Pharisees. Jesus spoke of God as ready to forgive and give His gift of righteousness to them, and so they came to Him, drawn by His Good News.

Going further, Jesus warned the Pharisees that the socially unacceptable would enter the kingdom before they would: "And I say to you, that many shall come from east and west, and recline at table with Abraham, and Isaac, and Jacob, in the kingdom of heaven; but the sons of the kingdom shall be cast out into the outer darkness; in that place there shall be weeping and gnashing of teeth" (Matthew 8:11-12).

The Gentiles from east and west, as well as tax gatherers, were very ready to come helplessly to receive God's gift and so enter the kingdom. The proud Pharisee stood aloof, not willing to admit his works were not enough to satisfy God's awful holiness.

The Good News that righteousness was given as a gift from God was most clearly taught in a story Jesus told concerning a Pharisee and a tax gatherer:

> "Two men went up into the temple to pray, one a Pharisee, and the other a tax-gatherer.
>
> "The Pharisee stood and was praying thus to himself, 'God, I thank Thee that I am not like other people: swindlers, unjust, adulterers, or even like this tax-gatherer.
>
> 'I fast twice a week; I pay tithes of all that I get.'
>
> "But the tax-gatherer, standing some distance away, was even unwilling to lift up his eyes to heaven, but was beating his breast, saying, 'God, be merciful to me, the sinner!'
>
> "I tell you, this man went down to his house justified rather than the other; for every one who exalts himself shall be humbled, but he who humbles himself shall be exalted."
>
> Luke 18:10-14

The Pharisee, seeking to establish his own right-eousness, missed acceptance with God. Whereas the tax gatherer threw himself on the mercy of God and found he was forgiven, made righteous, and accepted.

These who would be in His kingdom, righteous with God's righteousness, Jesus called "blessed ones." The word, *blessing*, is a rich word meaning joy, rest, total peace—such joy as to make a man the envy of all who know him. The words "blessed ones" take in all that the prophets had said about those who lived in Zion under Messiah.

At the end of some of His stories Jesus described the result of receiving God's gift as hilarious joy. He has the prodigal's father saying, "And bring the fattened calf, kill it, and let us eat and be merry; for this son of mine was dead, and has come to life again; he was lost, and has been found" (Luke 15:23-24).

To stand before God, accepted through His gift, and to be able to walk through life, no longer searching or struggling, but resting in the right-eousness He gives, this is life. In a parable Jesus said, "Again, the kingdom of heaven is like a merchant seeking fine pearls, and upon finding one pearl of great value, he went and sold all that he had, and bought it" (Matthew 13:45-46).

To others, though they stumble on it—it becomes their passion and the beginning of a new life: "The kingdom of heaven is like a treasure hidden in the field, which a man found and hid; and from joy over it he goes and sells all that he has, and buys that field" (Matthew 13:44).

Jesus did not come to begin a new religion. He stated only what Moses and the prophets had said. He brought it to its greatest fulfillment in Himself and in the kingdom over which He reigned.

14

The King Who Washes Feet

The twelve men and Jesus reclined around the table. The air was cool but not cold. They were separated from the night outside by curtains that enclosed the flat roof of the house in Jerusalem. The curtains billowed and fell limp as the gentle wind blew from time to time.

Oil lamps sputtered, giving off a flickering yellow light and a thin wisp of smoke, casting giant moving shadows on the walls. The light fell on the faces of the twelve tense men, the inner circle of His followers. At this point, all but one of them believed they would die for Him.

There were Peter, James, and John. They had been fishing partners in Galilee before throwing in their nets and following Jesus. Peter—rough, coarse, loud, and unthinking, but the unquestionable leader of the group. James and John—John the teenager of the band—were both ready to burst into violent rage at the slightest pro-vocation. Jesus had called them *Sons of Thunder*.

Matthew had been a tax collector and had been called from his booth to become a devoted follower. Simon the Canaanite had trouble with that, for he was a member of the fanatical zealot party and would happily kill a Jew who had sold out to Rome. They maintained a tense peace as followers of the One who called them both. Thomas was the deepest of the twelve, the most hardheaded realist, but for all his caution was probably the only one who had faced up to what it meant to die with Jesus. That is why he was at the table that night. Then there was Judas. He had never really fitted the group; coming from Judea, unlike the others, he seemed to be the odd one out. Tonight he shrank back into the shadows, his dark eyes darting up and down the table.

The Passover had begun at six o'clock that night. Jesus had sent Peter and John ahead to prepare the meal, observing the custom practiced since Israel had become a nation. The meal they were about to eat was kept secret from the thousands who would otherwise have been sitting outside. It was a calm before the storm that must break soon.

Judas drew further back into the shadows. Soon he had to slip out, and he didn't want anyone watching his going. It seemed all eyes were on him tonight. He had to go through with it; he was committed now. A few days ago he had stood before Caiaphas. He had been blunt, knowing that he was despised by the priests for what he was doing: "What are you willing to give me to deliver Him up to you?' And they weighed out to him thirty pieces of silver. And from then on he began looking for a good opportunity to betray Him" (Matthew 26:15-16).

Tonight was the night, and as soon as he was sure Jesus would be in Gethsemane, he would be going to Caiaphas to make arrangements.

A little over a week ago the group had returned to Bethany for a supper with Lazarus, only to find the village overrun with visitors who wanted to see not only Jesus but also Lazarus, the man Jesus had raised from death. At that news, the Sanhedrin had decided to kill Lazarus, too, afraid that he might continue the movement when they had finished with Jesus.

They had gone into Jerusalem from Bethany at the beginning of Passover week. Jesus rode on the foal of a donkey, the coats of devoted disciples forming the saddle. The route was lined with waving, cheering, laughing, crying Galileans and Jews alike. They pulled branches from the palm trees and threw them on His path, making a green carpet on which to ride. They shouted, "Hosanna! BLESSED IS HE WHO COMES IN THE NAME OF THE LORD, even the King of Israel" (John 12:13).

As they crested the Mount of Olives and came down into Jerusalem the mountainside was a seething mass of people—all rejoicing, shouting, acclaiming Him as Messiah, true King of Israel, Shiloh who was to come.

Some undoubtedly remembered the prophet's words:

> Rejoice greatly, O daughter of Zion!
> Shout in triumph, O daughter of Jerusalem!
> Behold, your king is coming to you;

141

> He is just and endowed with salvation,
> Humble, and mounted on a donkey,
> Even on a colt, the foal of a donkey.
>> Zechariah 9:9

In the thrill of the moment, the disciples caught sight of a group of priests watching malignantly from the gate of the city. A cold chill went through them, momentarily dispersing their triumph. Either He would declare Himself king, or those priests would act.

The last week had seen a heightening of a tension that already was ready to snap. Again Jesus had emptied the Bazaar of the sons of Annas of its money changers and priests, accusing them of being thieves and robbers in religious guise.

Now the men sat with the emotion of the triumphant entry and the fear of the pure hate they had seen in the cold, merciless eyes of some of the chief priests in the temple courts that very week. They were edgy and snappy.

But the atmosphere was caused not only by enemies. A bitter quarrel seethed just below the surface. In a sense it had always been there, erupting into the open every so often. It hinged on the questions: Who *was the greatest? Who was closest to Jesus?* In the kingdom about to be set up, who would reign along with Jesus, who would be heads of state? At times their arguments became violent. He had often rebuked them, saying that the leaders of His kingdom were the servants of all, but they had not heard Him.

Tonight, Peter and John had made all the arrangements for the Passover—all but for one item.

Neither of them would stoop to it, any more than any one of the remaining ten would. As guests entered a house it was customary for their feet to be bathed, washing the dust and soreness away. It was a simple act, but a menial task reserved for the lowest servant. Each of these men aspired to political office in a kingdom about to burst upon the world. They jostled one another to prove their superiority and closeness to Messiah. Each thought the other should be washing feet.

By the time they sat down, no one's feet had been washed. Although no one mentioned it, the anger was in everyone's voice like faraway thunder. Then it happened:

> Jesus, knowing that the Father had given all things into His hands, and that He had come forth from God, and was going back to God,
>
> rose from supper, and laid aside His garments; and taking a towel, girded Himself about.
>
> Then He poured water into the basin, and began to wash the disciples' feet, and to wipe them with the towel with which He was girded.
>
> John 13:3-5

Peter watched aghast. They knew who He was. They had confessed Him as the Messiah, the Christ, the Son of the living God—the deliverer promised from the dawn of history. He was the descendant of Abraham, son of David, born to be king over earth, Lord of heaven, God with us. *And He was washing their feet!*

Peter's thoughts raced wildly. That isn't the way to rule over men, that isn't power! Caesar doesn't wash the feet of his soldiers, not even his centurions. Power means they wash *his* feet! Power means they cringe before him and obey. *What is Jesus doing?*

Jesus came to Judas. He met his shifting gaze, and kneeling before him, removed his sandals and gently bathed his feet. Judas looked at the One the others called Messiah, kneeling before him as a slave and nearly burst into tears.

Peter was horrified as he pursued his thoughts. *What kind of kingdom is this going to be if this is its power?* The king of the earth washes the feet of slaves? A king who serves His slaves? If the king served His subjects in His rule over them, *what kind of relationship are the subjects supposed to have to one another?* It all seemed so foolish.

> And so He came to Simon Peter. He said to Him, "Lord, do You wash my feet?"
>
> Jesus answered and said to him, "What I do you do not realize now; but you shall understand hereafter."
>
> Peter said to Him, "Never shall You wash my feet!" Jesus answered him, "If I do not wash you, you have no part with Me."
>
> Simon Peter said to Him, "Lord, not my feet only, but also my hands and head."
>
> Jesus said to him, "He who has bathed needs only to wash his feet, but is completely clean; and you are clean, but not all of you." For He knew the one who was betraying Him; for this reason He said, "Not all of you are clean."
>
> John 13:6-11

144

They took their places at the table. Their damp, cool feet condemned their pride and preached at them from beneath the table. An awe was on them as they felt their ideas of kingdom disintegrate, but still not grasping that they had beheld true power. And Jesus said to them:

"Do you know what I have done to you?

"You call Me Teacher and Lord; and you are right; for so I am.

"If I then, the Lord and the Teacher, washed your feet, you also ought to wash one another's feet.

"For I gave you an example that you also should do as I did to you.

"Truly, truly, I say to you, a slave is not greater than his master; neither one who is sent greater than the one who sent him.

"If you know these things, you are blessed if you do them."

John 13:12-17

"The kings of the Gentiles lord it over them; and those who have authority over them are called 'Benefactors.'

"But not so with you, but let him who is the greatest among you become as the youngest, and the leader as the servant.

"For who is greater, the one who reclines at table, or the one who serves? Is it not the one who reclines at table? But I am among you as the one who serves."

Luke 22:25-27

A shadow passed across the Lord's face. It was noticeable to all, like the shadow of an approaching agony. His gaze met their inquiring eyes. He said hoarsely, "Truly, truly, I say to you, that one of you will betray Me" (John 13:21).

Their mouths fell open. They may argue for first place, but their argument was at least in part because of their devotion to Him. It was unthinkable that any one of them should betray Him. They asked Him in shocked whispers, "Lord, is it I?" They talked low among themselves.

Dipping the bread into the gravy, He handed it to Judas. Their eyes met. Judas earnestly asked, "Lord, it isn't me you are talking about, is it?" There was enough conversation that the disciples didn't hear Jesus say, "You have said it yourself—what you do, do quickly." (See Matthew 26:25 and John 13:27.)

Judas took the morsel and swallowed it, sitting back. A hideous darkness settled on him. He had looked in the eyes of Messiah, serving Him and honoring Him, and he chose to sell Him to the priests. Satan entered him and he went into the night to find Caiaphas to make final arrangements. Some had heard Jesus tell him to be quick, and had supposed that as treasurer he had an errand to perform. After Judas went out the conversation picked up; it seemed a cloud had lifted, though they knew not why.

At a certain point in the Passover meal the host broke a piece of the unleavened bread and shared it around. Jesus as host broke the matzo and then surprised everyone with the words, "This is My body which is given for you; do this in remem-brance of Me" (Luke 22:19). His body given for them? A broken body? Messiah with a broken body? Puzzled, they held their peace.

146

After they had eaten He took the cup of wine and held it. "This cup which is poured out for you is the new covenant in My blood" (Luke 22:20).

The words shocked them. His blood poured out for them? But their shock was overlaid by the thrill of the words *new covenant*. They knew enough to recognize the words of Jeremiah the Prophet. The new covenant, the new relationship of the new age of Messiah. In that new relationship, sin and iniquity would be remembered no more, and God's Law would be written on the heart of a person.

What they did not yet understand, however, was that if it was a *new* covenant, then the one they had lived under and by for two thousand years would be *old*. If old, then ready to be replaced by the new one. The promises would come to fulfillment. The shadows would come to reality in the new covenant of which He spoke.

It meant that Israel as a nation had come to the end of the task it had embarked on at the ratifying of the covenant that Jesus had just declared as *old*. That old covenant was its charter as a nation, and it had just been declared old, superseded by the new covenant. Not that Israel would be cast aside—rather caught up, fulfilled, to become a higher kind of nation, enjoying all that God had ever promised and shadowed in them.

The temple and its sacrifices would be needed no more. The new covenant was in His blood and would bring about a state where sin and iniquity would be remembered no more. The animal sacrifices of the old covenant were continual sacrifices, for sin was never taken away. This sacrifice He spoke of would deal with sin forever, doing away with the need of temple and bloody sacrifice.

But under the sputtering yellow light of the little oil lamps, the eleven men seated around the Messiah did not realize for one moment the implication of what He had said. Nor would they fully see it all for months, even years, to come. Traditions die hard. A new day doesn't dawn all at once—and these words were the first ray of light.

They did not think for one minute that within seventy-two hours the new day of Messiah that prophets had sung of for centuries would be here.

They still believed He would proclaim Himself as king tonight.

15

Confused Disciples

The stone which the builders rejected
Has become the chief corner stone.
This is the Lord's doing;
It is marvelous in our eyes.
This is the day which the Lord has made;
Let us rejoice and be glad in it.
O Lord, do save, we beseech Thee;
O Lord, we beseech Thee, do send
prosperity!
Blessed is the one who comes in the
name of the Lord;
We have blessed you from the house of
the Lord.
The Lord is God, and He has given us
light;
Bind the festival sacrifice with cords to
the horns of the altar.
Thou art my God, and I give thanks to
Thee;
Thou art my God, I extol Thee.

> Give thanks to the Lord, for He is good;
> For His lovingkindness is everlasting.
>
> > Psalms 118:22-29

The rise and fall of twelve men chanting the *hallel* echoed faintly in the narrow street outside. It marked the end of the Passover meal for Jesus and the disciples.

As they prepared to go, Jesus told them that He was going away and, moreover, where He was going they could not come. Peter's voice rose in protest, "Lord, where are You going?"

Slowly Jesus shook His head and went on: "You will all fall away because of Me this night, for it is written, 'I WILL STRIKE DOWN THE SHEPHERD, AND THE SHEEP OF THE FLOCK SHALL BE SCATTERED.' But after I have been raised, I will go before you to Galilee" (Matthew 26:31-32).

Peter looked around at the others in the dim light. He was convinced that none of them could love Jesus more than he did. Any one of them was capable of failing Messiah, leaving Him when He needed them most, but he was sure he never could. He took in the table with a glance and said with a voice swollen with confidence, "Even though all may fall away because of You, I will never fall away" (Matthew 26:33).

Now Jesus deliberately addressed Peter by his old name Simon, who would disown a friend for the smile of the crowd. Simon with no courage or willpower, just wild, blustering talk, craving acceptance in his words. In that name Peter faced himself as he was apart from the life-change the presence of Messiah made. He reddened under his Galilean tan and cast his eyes down.

"Simon, Simon, behold, Satan has demanded permission to sift you like wheat; but I have prayed for you, that your faith may not fail; and you, when once you have turned again, strengthen your brothers" (Luke 22: 31-32). Peter protested. Wasn't Jesus aware of his devotion? If anyone deserved to go with Him to His ultimate triumph, surely it would be he; yet now Jesus singled him out as an object of special prayer.

Jesus looked deeply into the hurt eyes of this blustering disciple and asked, "Will you lay down your life for Me? Truly, truly, I say to you, a cock shall not crow, until you deny Me three times" (John 13:38). Everyone gasped. Peter wanted to shout a thousand contradictions, but the Lord's look of awful solemnity made the words stick in his throat.

Jesus did not pursue the statement, but went right on: "Let not your heart be troubled; believe in God, believe also in Me" (John 14:1). Among the kingdoms of the world a position of honor was earned by loyalty. Peter faced the One he owned as David's son, Shiloh, Messiah, the King, who was solemnly telling him that his disloyalty was to gain him a special place of prayer and care from His king.

The theme was picked up where it had begun before the disturbing prophecy. He was leaving them. Now He began to tell them why He was going:

> "In My Father's house are many dwelling places; if it were not so, I would have told you; for I go to prepare a place for you.

"And if I go and prepare a place for you,
I will come again, and receive you to Myself;
that where I am, there you may be also.

"And you know the way where I am
going."

John 14:2-4

They had watched Jesus under all circumstances for three years now, and His constant awareness of the Father had been His most outstanding characteristic. As devout Jews, they had associated the presence of God with the temple, especially the holy of holies—the Zion of David's holy hill. David had spoken of dwelling in the house of the Lord forever, and in Jesus they had seen the ultimate of consciously dwelling in the presence of the Father. They beheld His joy, peace, and walk within total acceptance by the Father. *What He had just said meant that they too would have a dwelling in the Father's house, even as they now beheld it in Him.* He was leaving them tonight to prepare the place for them to dwell within the Father's presence.

How did anyone get into that invisible domain called the Father's house? They knew He was not talking of the temple that was a few blocks from where they sat. "Thomas said to Him, 'Lord, we do not know where You are going; how do we know the way?'" (John 14:5).

All eyes turned to Jesus as He pointed to Himself and said, "I am the way, and the truth, and the life; no one comes to the Father, but through Me" (John 14:6).

The door into the invisible world of the Father's house was Jesus Messiah Himself. In the drinking of the cup of wine He had told them that He would effect the new covenant, which promised that within the covenant all men would *know* the Lord. By making the new covenant, Jesus Messiah would bring every person who believed into ultimate communion with the Father, dwelling in His house. This He would go and accomplish for them *tonight;* and having accomplished it, He would return to them that they might share a common life.

At that time they would be given a disclosure of the Father's love such as they had seen between Jesus and the Father. This disclosure of love would be unknown by the world, reserved for those who obeyed Jesus as Lord Messiah, doing all He commanded:

> "He who has My commandments and keeps them, he it is who loves Me; and he who loves Me shall be loved by My Father, and I will love him, and will disclose Myself to him.. . ."

> "If anyone loves Me, he will keep My word; and My Father will love him, and We will come to him, and make Our abode with him."

> John 14:21-23

Their eyes were heavy and the flickering lights had the effect of mesmerizing them. His words and explanations skimmed over their consciousness like mosquitoes over a lake on a summer night. They could not grasp what He was saying.

For Him to go to the Father would not only mean dynamic communion within the Father's love, but that on earth they would do the works He had done. For He had said:

> "Truly, truly, I say to you, he who believes in Me, the works that I do shall he do also; and greater works than these shall he do; because I go to the Father.
>
> "And whatever you ask in My name, that will I do, that the Father may be glorified in the Son.
>
> "If you ask Me anything in My name, I will do it."
>
> John 14:12-14

The result of their entering into the Father's presence as a dwelling place would mean that on earth Christ would be multiplied. They had watched Him perform miracles and had performed some themselves under His supervision. Now, because He was going away on their behalf, they would be His hands and feet on earth.

Outside, Jerusalem was quiet. A dog barked in the street below, and the Passover moon rode high in the sky, bathing the Judean countryside in its light. He seemed to be speaking of a world beyond this one. The tired men tried to fit what He was saying into the physical world they lived in. He then spoke of a special gift He would ask of the Father:

> "And I will ask the Father, and He will give you another Helper, that He may be with you forever;
>
> "that is the Spirit of truth, whom the world cannot receive, because it does not behold Him or know Him, but you know Him because He abides with you, and will be in you."
>
> John 14:16-17

154

It was John the Baptist who had first introduced the idea of the Spirit being the goal of Messiah's coming. He had equated the union of man with the Spirit to the kingdom of Messiah. That night He would leave them to establish His kingdom by making the Spirit available to men.

This would bring about an entirely new relationship between Him and His disciples. On that day He would be in them a vital life force. "In that day you shall know that I am in My Father, and you in Me, and I in you" (John 14:20).

Their minds, tired and heavy, spun wearily trying to grasp what tonight and the day of His return would mean. Jesus assured them that the One who was coming would bring all He said to them: "The Helper, the Holy Spirit, whom the Father will send in My name, He will teach you all things, and bring to your remembrance all that I said to you" (John 14:26).

Then, as if suddenly aware of an appointment to keep, He said, "Arise, let us go from here" (John 14:31).

The room had been hot and stuffy. The smoky lamps had made their eyes heavy. The air outside was like a cold shower and they stretched, inhaling its invigorating freshness. Jesus moved in the direction of the lower pool and the fountain gate, and they followed Him in twos and threes, discussing His words in low puzzled tones. Outside the gate they followed the narrow path that hugged the base of the east wall of the city. Eight feet below, the Kidron Brook was a sluggish trickle.

Across the brook, they passed the communities of Gihon and Siloam, swollen now with thousands of pilgrims from all over the Roman world who had come to Jerusalem for Passover. Tents covered the ground around the villages and the wall of the holy city. The camp fires of the thousands of pilgrims had burned low, casting a ruddy glow here and there. The smell of wood smoke hung on the night air.

Above them now were the great walls of Jerusalem, topped by the eastern view of Solomon's temple. The eastern facade carried a motif of grapes in solid gold four stories high. All was bathed and picked out by the brilliant moon.

The grapes were the most ancient symbol of Israel. The prophets had sung of Israel as God's vine, His chosen and cultivated plant, who, in its rebellion, had brought forth sour grapes. The psalmist had sung a dirge to God concerning His judgments on His vine:

> Thou didst remove a vine from Egypt;
> Thou didst drive out the nations, and didst plant it.
> Thou didst clear the ground before it,
> And it took deep root and filled the land.
> The mountains were covered with its shadow;
> And the cedars of God with its boughs.
> It was sending out its branches to the sea,
> And its shoots to the River.
> Why hast Thou broken down its hedges,
> So that all who pass that way pick its fruit?

A boar from the forest eats it away,
And whatever moves in the field feeds
on it.

Psalms 80:8-13

But over the wail of the psalmist was the promise of a new day for Israel, the vine of the Lord: "In the days to come Jacob will take root, Israel will blossom and sprout; And they will fill the whole world with fruit" (Isaiah 27:6). A day would come when Israel would be what God had ever intended—Israel would blossom and fill the earth with His glory. The temple grapes were the proud reminder to the Israelites that they were God's vine, destined to cover the earth.

Jesus said, "I am the true vine, and My Father is the vinedresser" (John 15:1). The *true* vine. What did that say of Israel, its multitudes now packed into every available place within and without the city? Was she not God's vine? In the man who stood on the path in the shadow of the temple wall was God's true vine. He had been before Israel from everlasting, and Israel was His shadow on earth, speaking of Him and predicting Him. Israel had broken the covenant and now lay under judgment.

Isaiah had described her: A stump of a tree that had fallen. He had gone on to say that out of that stump would come a shoot that eventually would become the whole tree. Here now was Jesus, the shoot out of David, the true Israel, and all who were united to Him would be members of the new Israel. These were the branches that would blossom and fill the earth:

157

> "Abide in Me, and I in you. As the branch cannot bear fruit of itself, unless it abides in the vine, so neither can you, unless you abide in Me.
>
> "I am the vine, you are the branches; he who abides in Me, and I in him, he bears much fruit; for apart from Me you can do nothing.
>
> "If anyone does not abide in Me, he is thrown away as a branch, and dries up; and they gather them, and cast them into the fire, and they are burned."
>
> John 15:4-6

It was new terminology and beyond their comprehension. The first days in Galilee He had called them to *follow Him.* To "follow" was a simple concept to understand—but now He spoke of *being united to Him.*

He was not only the way to the Father and the giver of the Spirit *but union with Him was the only way for a person to be a part of Messiah's Israel.* He would be living His life through them, even as vine life flowed through branches and produced grapes. They would not only do His works, but live His life.

They wrinkled their brows as they crossed Kidron Brook by the stone bridge and began the gradual ascent of the Mount of Olives. It was impossible for them to think of this physical Messiah who walked ahead of them as being *in* them.

Now He turned and spoke to them of love. The conversation had begun hours before on that note when He told them, "A new commandment I give to you, that you love one another" (see John 13:34-35).

158

But, the thought had been lost in the forecast of Peter's disowning Him. Now Jesus returned to it, describing the relationships that the subjects of this kingdom must have toward one another.

"This is My commandment, that you love one another, just as I have loved you. Greater love has no one than this, that one lay down his life for his friends" (John 15:12-13). Up to this point their love for each other was like that of a family of quarreling brothers. They were called to a new kind of love. The word Jesus used for love spoke of covenant love, faithful to the point of self-sacrifice and death for its object.

Each of these eleven men still lived in the fantasy that he was in the center of the universe. Their devotion to Jesus these last years had been muddied by their desire for personal glory by association with Him. With self in the center of their world, no one else could be truly loved, only *self*. His word for love called them to a selfless kind of love they had never known before. By this they would be marked as the subjects of Messiah, the original lover.

They turned around and looked at the city now below them with its pinpoints of dancing lights and the occasional glow of a pilgrim fire. Jesus knew that inside that city, the lord of darkness—the pretend ruler of the planet earth—had entered into Judas to engineer the death of Messiah. Even now, Judas was with the temple guards who were rounding up the servants of Annas who hung around the temple courts and the priests who wanted to be in on the kill. Soon he would lead them to arrest the One he once thought was Messiah.

Up on the hill Jesus turned to the eleven men straggling behind Him. He knew that, although within hours the kingdom would come into being, it would be generations before its consummation. Although living in the Father's house, enjoying His love, in union with Messiah, the true Israel, and doing His works on earth, they would be pressured and bitterly persecuted by the world. As He lived within them and they obeyed Him in His power, the world would treat them as He knew it would treat Him tonight.

> "If the world hates you, you know that it has hated Me before it hated you.
> "If you were of the world, the world would love its own; but because you are not of the world, but I chose you out of the world, therefore the world hates you.
> "Remember the word that I said to you, 'A slave is not greater than his master. . . .'"
> John 15:18-20

His words fell harshly on their ears. They had thought of His kingdom arriving in an explosion of power and glory at the appearance of Messiah. The idea of a kingdom growing within the opposition of enemies was foreign to them. They had not heard Daniel saying that a stone cut without hands would *gradually fill* the earth, nor the psalmists that spoke of Messiah being crowned in spite of the raging nations, of His reign *in the midst of His enemies*.

Worse yet, the Israel, the ancient nation of the old covenant, was to be the vanguard of the persecution. The new-covenant Israel of Messiah was going to be expelled from the old-covenant Israel.

> "These things I have spoken to you, that you may be kept from stumbling.
> "They will make you outcasts from the synagogue; but an hour is coming for everyone who kills you to think that he is offering service to God.
> "And these things they will do, because they have not known the Father, or Me."
>
> John 16:1-3

They would cling to their false hopes of national glory instead of understanding that the glory the prophets had spoken of was acknowledging Jesus as Messiah the Lord and living in the Spirit with Him. In such a theater of hatred they were to witness to Messiah and be His heralds. Again He urged the tired, heavy-lidded disciples to remember that in that day all their ability would be in the Spirit:

> "I have many more things to say to you, but you cannot hear them now.
> "But when He, the Spirit of truth, comes, He will guide you into all the truth; for He will not speak on His own initiative, but whatever He hears, He will speak; and He will disclose to you what is to come.
> "He shall glorify Me; for He shall take of Mine, and shall disclose it to you."
>
> John 16:12-14

They were now standing under the olive trees in the garden of Gethsemane, nearly half a mile from

Jerusalem. The smell of stale olive oil hung heavy on the air from the nearby presses. The moon cast dark shadows on the darker earth; the gray leaves were silver in the pools of light.

He motioned them to sit. They slumped against the gnarled trunks, trying to keep their eyes open. He was saying it again—He was going away and they would experience sorrow and pain. It would be like the sorrow accompanying a baby's birth, followed by joy.

Looking over them He repeated the awful words, "Behold, an hour is coming, and has already come, for you to be scattered, each to his own home, and to leave Me alone; and yet I am not alone, because the Father is with Me" (John 16:32). And then with triumph in His voice that entered into their hearts like a fire, "These things I have spoken to you, that in Me You may have peace. In the world you have tribulation, but take courage; I have overcome the world" (John 16:33).

Peter stifled a yawn and Matthew found his eyes closing against his will. Jesus said, "Sit here while I go over there and pray" (Matthew 26:36).

16

"Thy Will Be Done"

The grove was darker now, and the shadows cast by the moon larger. The Messiah turned and walked into the trees—Peter, James, and John followed Him. He turned and looked at them. They started visibly at what they saw.

Tonight the moon shone on haggard features and threw into relief a look of fear that caused the three men to hesitate in their tracks. Fleetingly one of them recollected the fear of utter loneliness when lost as a child. The face of Messiah reflected such a sense of desertion and aloneness. Then He said to them, "My soul is deeply grieved, to the point of death." The sorrow was surrounding Him, tightening its grip like a vise and seeking to crush Him to death here under the trees. "Remain here and keep watch with Me" (Matthew 26:38).

He walked away from them about as far as a man could throw a stone and fell prostrate in an agony of prayer. The hour He had spoken of all His life had come. An hour in which time and eternity met.

The night slid by, the hours marked off by the procession of stars and moon across the sky. The monotonous dirge of insects in orchestra was slowly dying out as a breeze began to stir the silver leaves.

Before the vastness of space was created in its cocoon of time and before suns and planets hung in it or trees and insects covered and swarmed the earth, He who lay in the sod had chosen the path that led to this moment of decision. He was the only man who *was* before He was born, who had in fact chosen to be born, that He might choose to die.

He who always was God the Son, had chosen to take real human nature in the womb of the Virgin Mary. So perfect and complete was the choice to assume our humanity that the babe who had clung to the young mother did not know more than any other newborn babe. He had chosen to be true man, and therefore did not know He had chosen. In that decision before time, He had chosen to be the sent One of the Father, to enter the creation to bring rebel humanity back to the Father.

Because of that purpose of the Godhead, the promise of a deliverer was given. Before man first looked around in self-consciousness and before he sinned, God had determined to enter the race to deliver the people. It was that eternal will of the Father to send the Son that was the ground of the prophets' words that sin and iniquity would be remembered no more. It would be done, for God was coming to earth to accomplish it. That decision had always meant He would, as man, choose to die.

The eternal purpose of the Godhead was now being lived out in man's history, while frogs called to each other in the Kidron Brook. The horror of what it meant came upon Him. The choice made in eternity was now being accepted and experienced in the frailty of His manhood. Surveying what it meant He cried out, "My Father, if it is possible, let this cup pass from Me; yet not as I will, but as Thou wilt" (Matthew 26:39).

He rose from the ground and went back to the disciples. They were slumped against each other around the gnarled roots of a tree, their striped robes pulled around them against the breeze. He said to Peter, "Simon are you asleep? Could you not keep watch for one hour? Keep watching and praying, that you may not come into temptation; the spirit is willing, but the flesh is weak'" (Mark 14:37-38). Peter winced. Ready to die for Him, but asleep when He needed them. Through leaden eyes they watched Him go into the shadows again with the restlessness of a great burden on Him. *Was this the Messiah?* Who would believe it?

As He knelt again to pray, the burden on Him increased in a horror of fear, loneliness, and anticipated desertion by His Father and followers.

A few miles away tens of thousands of pilgrims waited anxiously for Messiah to appear. On the way to Jerusalem they had shared excitedly whether or not at this feast He would suddenly come into the temple in a burst of flaming light. In the Tower of Antonia, the Roman fortress that dominated Jerusalem and overlooked the temple, the midnight guards stamped their feet and blew into their cold hands. Extra troops brought in from Caesarea slept below. At every feast the Roman garrison was prepared in case some madman led a revolt, thinking he was the Messiah.

Neither the devoted Israelite praying for David's son to appear nor the wary Roman soldiers would have looked twice at the bowed figure sweating in fear beneath the trees. The words of Isaiah hung unspoken on the air, "Who has believed our message? And to whom has the arm of the Lord been revealed?" (Isaiah 53:1).

A suffering Messiah! Was this the glorious king? But there was no other way to achieve what God had willed in His holiness.

His being is ever opposed to sin. Sin was not something that annoyed Him but could be tolerated. He was opposed to it with the totality of His being. Sin must be judged and removed, for justice is the way He is. He loved man, yet how could He return to Himself the one who was wedded to sin and, so, the object of His wrath?

The Son was sent by the Father to take to Himself human nature, to live in that nature in all its limitations, be tempted in that nature, and sinless, vindicate the beauty of holiness. But He was to take that life and on behalf of all men offer it to the Father—to be the substitute for man, bearing the just wrath their sin deserved. When man would be forgiven it would be with holy forgiveness—not an amnesty in which God ignored sin, but holy forgiveness in which He Himself bore the sin.

When man sinned in actual history, the One who would take his place was ready. He had been ready since before the foundation of the ages. He would not yet come and deliver man, for sin had to come to its head—then He would deal with it in one blow, forever.

Until such a time, God had given man the way back to Himself in animal sacrifices. The shed blood of the animals sprinkled on the altar had no meaning unless founded on the covenant made between Father and Son. They had no hope in them except as they pointed forward to the day He would come and actually bear the sin of man. Man's blasphemous rebellion against God would be laid on this sinless One. He would become sin and enter into death, the darkness of the lie. The wrath of the Father against sin would focus on Him and be consumed. Man would be free from con-demnation through the blood shedding of the God-man Messiah Jesus.

The rivers of blood that had flowed from the veins of animals cut by priestly knives had all anticipated this hour. The Lamb who would give meaning to all sacrificial lambs now faced the final sacrifice to be made on planet earth.

Many men had chosen to die, but this One had chosen to put aside His rights as God and become as man in order to die. It was not dying that caused the horror of fear to enclose Him, *but death.* He was to take upon Himself the rebel man, the curse that was man's and Himself become the focus of divine wrath.

Death was avoided by all men, but the best of men carried death in their spirits. They had all embraced the lie inherited from father Adam and knew death from the hour of self-consciousness. *Death was man's concept of living.* When death finally swallowed up their bodies, it was the belated an-nouncement of a death that had long been a part of them. The physical dissolution was the feared and unwelcome consummation of what they had always known in embryo.

But this One was without sin and without death in His spotless spirit, soul, and body. And the thought of *becoming sin* on behalf of all men, taking death and embracing it to Himself, caused Him to recoil in horror. He who had eternally fellowshiped with the Father, and in His humanity had lived in total joy of His Father's love, was now to become the object of His Father's wrath.

The animals in the temple had no rational choice. The man who is to die for all men must *willingly* choose. His act must be the laying down of His life. His choice must be rooted in His seeing sin as God sees it, feeling the pain of it even as God does, and accepting the wrath of God against it and bearing it in His body.

His weak human nature shrank back from willing such an action that He had willed before He had human nature. The prophet had seen Him in a vision: "Surely our griefs He Himself bore, And our sorrows He carried; Yet we ourselves esteem-ed Him stricken, Smitten of God, and afflicted" (Isaiah 53:4). He drew back, feeling the black sorrow of such a moment, pressing and crushing Him from the future. Again He asked, "Father, if it is Your will, take this cup away from Me; nevertheless not My will, but Yours, be done."

He rose from his prayer and came again to the disciples. The snores and heavy breathing of the fishermen from Galilee rose and fell on the still night of Passover. The Messiah was alone. Alone He would defeat death by embracing it.

He left them asleep and went again to prayer. He was going into death for all men and would come out of it leaving it helplessly defeated. United to Him, millions would walk out of death into life, following Him to the Father's house, that where He was they would be also.

The agony of what He must do pressed upon Him, and He wrestled in awful contest. The sweat that ran like a river over His face and down His back began to change color—a light pink gradually turned to a deep red. Blood was seeping through the pores of His skin, streaking His face and falling in clots to the ground.

His free choice was made. On earth in time, a true man had freely chosen to obey the Father and, taking the place of all men, bear their sin and become the focus of the divine wrath man had earned. He had done so praising God that His will was right and holy and just.

The horrors of the next hours had been faced and triumphed over. In answer to His prayer, the father had sent angels to strengthen Him. His hair clung to His head, curling damply to His forehead. Drying blood matted His beard and colored the neckband of His robe.

He returned to his disciples and found them again asleep. "Are you still sleeping and taking your rest? Behold, the hour is at hand and the Son of Man is being betrayed into the hands of sinners. Arise, let us be going; behold, the one who betrays Me is at hand!'" (Matthew 26:45-46).

The men struggled to their feet, rubbing their eyes with their fists, staring stupidly at the sight of sovereign calm triumphantly shining through the devastation left by the agony.

17

Betrayed and Denied

In the shadow of the walls of Jerusalem a disorderly band of men moved toward the little bridge across the Kidron. Never had so many sworn enemies walked together, friends for a night by a common cause.

The pious Pharisees lifted their blue robes and picked their way across the stones, willing to put aside theological differences with the Sadducees to put the Nazarene to death. Caiaphas had gone to the Roman procurator earlier that night and explained that they needed soldiers to assist in the arrest of a man who was potentially dangerous. The Roman soldiers joked nervously about the night's work. They had heard many tales of this man, some even said He raised the dead. Certainly the priests were expecting some great show of power, or the soldiers would not have been called out.

Temple servants gripped their swords, the flickering torches casting a ruddy glow on their dark faces. They had a good reason to be in on the arrest. They had worked in the Bazaar of the sons of Annas and had been waiting to get even with the young rabbi. Tonight the tables would be turned on the Galilean, and they relished every moment of it.

At the head of the band hurried Judas. He wanted to get the night over with as quickly as possible. He had a nagging horror of what he was doing. Somewhere in the grove of trees ahead was the man he had followed for two years, confessing Him as Messiah. Disillusioned, he now led the priests like vultures to their prey. Thirty pieces of silver jingled in his leather purse.

The flaming torches cast giant shadows that danced among the trees as they entered the garden. Twigs cracked under foot, and branches tugged at fine blue robes. Soldiers cursed. Further in the trees, frightened disciples scrambled dizzily out of sleep, eyes darting in panic. Jesus stood regal, waiting for His captors.

Peter tightened his grip on his sword. He didn't usually carry one and was better at casting nets than sword fights with Romans. Tonight he was half asleep and trembling with fearful excitement.

The clearing was suddenly filled with men, vague and shadowy in the trees. The disciples were rooted to the spot. Then out of the shadows came Judas. No one knew why he was there or where he had come from, for all they knew he had already been arrested. He came directly to Jesus, threw his arms around Him with apparent joy and said, "Hail, Master."

Jesus looked sorrowfully at him: "Judas, are you betraying the Son of Man with a kiss?" (Luke 22:48), and then said to the hesitant mob behind him, "Whom do you seek?" (John 18:4).

The leader spoke with authority. They had come to arrest Jesus the Nazarene.

"I am He" (John 18:5). The three words Jesus spoke identified Him as the one they sought. But it was also the sacred name of the God of Israel. The speaking of the name hit the band of men like a hammer and they found themselves helpless on the ground. Embarrassed, they scrambled to their feet. Again Jesus asked, "Whom do you seek?" They said shakily, "Jesus the Nazarene" (*see* John 18:7). He addressed the temple crowd: "Have you come out with swords and clubs as against a robber? While I was with you daily in the temple, you did not lay hands on Me; but this hour and the power of darkness are yours" (Luke 22:52-53).

Peter fingered the hilt of his sword. It was time to fight, not talk. His devotion to Jesus needed to have arms put to it. He drew his sword and swung it in an arc toward the skull of one of Caiaphas' servants, Malchus by name. Peter missed his skull and scythed the man's ear. The man screamed as warm blood trickled down his neck. The Romans drew their swords and prepared to use them.

Jesus looked sternly at Peter and said, "Stop! No more of this" (Luke 22:51). Then He reached out His hand and laid it over the bloody mess that had been Malchus' ear. The servant of Annas became aware that the pain was gone and the bleeding had stopped.

The Romans were confused. They had been brought out to arrest a dangerous man in the middle of the night. Rumor had it that He might use magic on them. Instead, He ordered His followers not to fight and administered some kind of healing to one who openly hated Him.

They stepped forward and arrested Him. Hands tied painfully behind His back, Jesus was led by a rope to the house of the high priest.

The Roman soldiery was disappointed. Some Messiah! No one had been struck dead, no fire had been called from heaven, and even His followers had fled at the first threat from the soldiers. He now willingly went down the path with not even a murmur. He hadn't even cursed them. One of them spat into the woods and cursed Caiaphas for dragging them out to arrest a harmless weakling.

The door to the courtyard of the high priest's house opened to the soldiers, and they swarmed in with Jesus between Roman guards. House servants came with lanterns to get a glimpse of the One who had intimidated the temple authorities. They were disappointed. He looked a very usual kind of man, tired and with dried blood on His face. They looked at each other and laughed. A man as ordinary as that could not have raised the dead, let alone be the Messiah. He didn't even look like a god; His claims were not worth thinking about.

Peter and John had not fled with the other disciples but had followed the arrested Messiah at a healthy distance. Now they stood outside the gate to the high priest's residence, debating and shivering in the chill wind and from fear of where this might end.

John had done business with the high priest for his father, Zebedee, and knew some of the servants. He was sure he could get inside and probably bring Peter in, so they could find out what was happening. At his knock, a girl came to the door and lifted her lantern to shine in his face. She greeted him cordially when she saw who it was.

Peter stood in the shadows and watched as John was admitted. Inside, John took in the situation. The soldiers sat around a fire joking and throwing dice while servants hurried importantly across the courtyard. No one seemed to recognize John as a disciple of the Messiah who had now been led to Caiaphas in another part of the house. He decided it seemed safe enough. He went back to the girl and asked if she would let in a friend who was outside.

The door to the courtyard opened and the lantern shed a pool of light into the narrow street outside. Peter was summoned to come in. The light shone full in his face and the girl innocently asked, "Are you one of that man's disciples?"

Peter's mouth went dry and his throat tightened. Turning he said angrily, "I am not" (Luke 22:58). John looked at him, pained and horrified, but said nothing. They both joined the soldiers and servants around the fire and thankfully warmed themselves.

The members of the Great Sanhedrin had been summoned and were arriving every few minutes at the residence of Caiaphas. It was illegal to hold trial at night, but tonight they rationalized. The blasphemer had to be put to death quickly before the eight days of Passover were upon them, when no death sentence could be passed. It had to be done so quickly that His followers would not riot. A blasphemer could hardly expect justice, they rationalized. The only members of the council liable to throw the Law at Caiaphas were the Pharisees, but tonight they were friends.

18

Trial by Mockery

Peter stood with his head down, the ruddy glow of the fire keeping his head in shadow. John was silent in the shadows. One of the servants of Annas talked, retelling the story of the raid on the garden. It was a relative of Malchus, and he was making the most of being related to the only significant action that had taken place there. Suddenly he stopped and stared hard at Peter. "Did I not see you in the garden with Him?" (John 18:26). Wild-eyed, Peter shook his head, "Man, I was not there."

The Sanhedrin had gathered in the house of Caiaphas at the tables set in a crescent shape. It was no shock to them to be called, for the council had spoken of little else in the last weeks. The illegal trial was now under way.

Nicodemus stood there with downcast eyes to avoid the look of the Galilean he had interviewed and followed secretly ever since. He was ashamed to be part of the mockery of the law that this trial constituted. But he said nothing. Another secret follower of Jesus, Joseph of Arimathea, looked at the floor and fiddled with the tassels of his robe.

The mock trial got under way. As there were no witnesses to defend, the witnesses to accuse were brought in. They were the servants of Annas from the Bazaar. They swore they told the truth, but under the questions of the judges the necessary two agreeing could not be found. Collapsing under questioning they were dismissed as liars. Finally Caiaphas had two to agree that they had heard Him say He would rebuild the temple in three days. It was hardly a crime and certainly not worthy of death by Roman law.

Caiaphas looked at the accused. "Have You nothing to say?"

Through red, tired eyes Jesus looked back at Caiaphas. He said nothing. Caiaphas pressed: "Do You make no answer? What is it that these men are testifying against You?" (Matthew 26:62). Nicodemus cringed in disgust. There was no evidence! All the court had proved so far was that there was no testimony against Him.

The high priest was trapped. No evidence, and therefore no vote. The carefully hatched plan would collapse before it even got under way. He knew that the Sanhedrin wanted His death, but they were honest enough that they could not condemn Him to death with no evidence.

Caiaphas turned to Jesus in desperation: "I adjure You by the living God, that You tell us whether You are the Christ, the Son of God" (Matthew 26:63).

It was a shot in the dark hour of despair. The prisoner had not answered before; why should He answer now? He knew as well as they did that if He

178

didn't answer they would have to set Him free. To
the amazement of Caiaphas, He answered:

> "If I tell you, you will by no means
> believe.
> "And if I also ask you, you will by no
> means answer Me or let Me go.
> "Hereafter the Son of Man will sit on the
> right hand of the power of God."
> Then they all said, "Are You then the
> Son of God?" So He said to them, "You
> rightly say that I am."
>
> Luke 22:67-70, NKJV

Incredible! The high priest was elated. The
prisoner condemned Himself, quoting directly from
Daniel's ancient prophecy, claiming to be the
Messiah and about to be crowned the Lord of the
universe. He must be mad to blaspheme in the
presence of the whole court. Caiaphas dismissed
the law that said the words of the prisoner were not
to be taken into account, for these words were his
only hope of a death penalty.

Placing his hands on the high collar of his own
high priest's robe, he pulled, ripping the cloth. "He
has blasphemed! What further need do we have
of witnesses? Behold, you have now heard the
blasphemy; what do you think?" (Matthew 26:65-66).

There was no vote to be taken in the illegal
court—but they chorused, "He is deserving of
death!" (Matthew 26:66).

The court adjourned until dawn, when they
could legally meet in the light of day at the temple.
The judges of the supreme court of Israel rose from

their chairs. Anger and rage for this one who claimed to be Messiah rose within them like an uncontrollable flood. They desired His death—now. The most venerated men in Israel came and spat in His face and beat Him with their clenched fists.

The fire in the courtyard was burning low and conversation lulled. Soldiers asked impatiently what was going on in the house of Caiaphas. How much longer had they to sit and wait? Someone threw a log on the fire, and flames crept up the dry bark.

On the wall a rooster opened its eyes and stretched its neck. Ruffling its wings, it stood and strutted on the wall. Stretching its neck again, it crowed loudly.

One of the servants of Annas had been staring at Peter from the time he joined the group and now spoke boldly to the big fisherman clearly visible in the light of the fire: "Surely you are one of them, for you are a Galilean too." But he [Peter] began to curse and swear, "I do not know this fellow you are talking about!" (Mark 14:70-71).

Hardly had the awful oaths struck the air when the cock crowed a second time, long and loudly. Immediately the words of Jesus came back to Peter: "Before a cock crows twice, you will deny Me three times." And he began to weep (Mark 14:72).

They were leading Jesus from the house of Caiaphas at that moment. He was bent from the blows, His face puffed and bruised, the spittle of the Pharisees dripping from His beard. He turned, and in the firelight His eyes met the face of Peter. The blaspheming disciple looked in horror, then turned and ran from the courtyard, crying loudly with deep, convulsive sobs.

With no orders as to what they should do with Jesus, the soldiers and servants of the high priest gathered around Him and began to mock Him. They were bold now that they had seen He would not call fire from heaven. One, more bold than the others, clenched his fist and hit Him across the face. Another hit Him from the other side. They spat in His face, adding their saliva to that of the priests and judges. Someone took a towel and blindfolded Him. "Prophesy, who is the one who hit You?" (Luke 22:64). A fist that he could not see coming and thereby lessen the force of by moving His head, smashed into His mouth.

It was dawning, and the Great Sanhedrin were to meet at the first ray of sun, which would constitute a legal court. There would be no discussion, only the confirming of the illegal decision. The soldiers took Jesus through the grey pre-dawn streets to the temple. It was Passover, and happy worshipers were already moving toward the sacred courts. It is doubtful that anyone could have recognized the swollen purple face as that of Messiah Jesus, but the soldiers shielded Him from any curious eyes. If His followers from Galilee found out what had transpired in the night, there would be a riot.

In the Hall of Polished Stones within the temple, the members of the Great Sanhedrin took their place in the three rows shaped in a semicircle. It would be safe to say that Nicodemus and Joseph of Arimathea were not in the session. The other seats were filled with tired, irritable men. The court was a mockery called to confirm the illegal decision of the trial by night.

Each one stood and voted with the words, "He is guilty. Death." The clerk of the court wrote His name, the charge, and the sentence. This would be taken to the Roman governor for his approval.

That was the most difficult part of the affair. Caiaphas and Pilate detested each other. To Caiaphas, the governor was an unclean Gentile, human vermin defiling the holy city with his presence. Pilate looked upon the high priest as a scheming Jew who plotted his political downfall by placing him in impossible situations. He had loaned him the soldiers—but after that it would be a game of political chess. It pleased Pilate to know the wily priest could not achieve the death of this peasant without his approval, and he planned to make it difficult.

Jesus was led to the Tower of Antonia, situated on the edge of the city, its great double arches opening into the temple's Court of the Gentiles.

Already the courtyard was filled with worshipers, as many as thirty thousand thronging it. Many were asking where the prophet of Nazareth was. They had brought their sick, for they were sure He would be in the temple this day to heal and teach. They didn't recognize Him as the bent, exhausted prisoner closely guarded and surrounded by a mob led by the chief of priests and elders of the Sanhedrin.

The priests refused to go into the tower but stood on the temple side of the arches. They would not defile themselves before the Lord by entering a Gentile house. A message was sent to Pilate that Caiaphas was here.

The Roman in his toga and sandals curled his lip in disdain at the Jews gathered at the arches. They would not enter the tower and defile themselves, but they could deliver a poor fool from the hills out of envy because He was more popular than they. He asked them, "What accusation do you bring against this Man?" (John 18:29).

A strange question—surely he understood. Caiaphas tightened. So the governor was making the first move in being difficult. He hurled back sarcastically, "If this Man were not an evildoer, we would not have delivered Him up to you" (John 18:30).

Pilate hated the mock piety of the priest. He knew well that Caiaphas would very quickly hand over an innocent man for trial. Outwardly Pilate shrugged. "Take Him yourselves, and judge Him according to your law."

The Jews replied, "We are not permitted to put any one to death" (John 18:31).

Pilate was enjoying the game. Caiaphas was losing right now. In moments he would declare Jesus free, and Caiaphas would have every Jew in the nation around his ears. Knowing this, they accused Jesus, saying: "We found this man misleading our nation and forbidding to pay taxes to Caesar, and saying that He himself is Christ, a King" (Luke 23:2).

The words electrified Pilate. Some religious nonsense about a man who thought he was god he could play games with. This accusation was different. A king who had plans to set up a kingdom brought the empire into it. If he set this man free,

183

and Caiaphas contacted the emperor Tiberius, then Pilate would be recalled to Rome in disgrace and worse.

Pilate ordered Jesus to be brought to him. Inside the Praetorium the servants drew close to the man who had been everyone's topic of conversation in the last year. A wonder-worker who claimed He was God? They looked at the badly beaten peasant and snickered. Some Messiah who let Himself get into that state!

Pilate looked into the bruised and puffy face and asked:

> "Are You the King of the Jews?"
>
> Jesus answered him, "Are you speaking for yourself on this, or did others tell you this about Me?"
>
> Pilate answered, "Am I a Jew? Your own nation and the chief priests have delivered You to me. What have You done?"
>
> Jesus answered, "My kingdom is not of this world. If My kingdom were of this world, My servants would fight, so that I should not be delivered to the Jews; but now My kingdom is not from here."
>
> Pilate therefore said to Him, "Are You a king then?" Jesus answered, "You say rightly that I am a king. For this cause I was born, and for this cause I have come into the world, that I should bear witness to the truth. Everyone who is of the truth hears My voice."
>
> John 18:33-37, NKJV

Pilate then came out to the mob lusting for blood and solemnly announced, "I find no guilt in this man" (Luke 23:4).

Caiaphas felt his world slipping away. If Pilate freed Jesus they may as well close the temple. In desperation he said, "He stirs up the people, teaching all over Judea, starting from Galilee, even as far as this place" (Luke 23:5).

At the mention of Galilee, Pilate visibly brightened. He almost smiled. Galilee was Herod's territory, as Judea was Caiaphas'. Both were under Pilate. There had been severe disagreement between Herod and Pilate over an incident in the temple some time before. The unknown Galilean would be the pawn in a political move. He would send the prisoner to Herod as a gesture of friendship, honoring the puppet king by putting the case in his hands. Herod was a Jew, and if he gave Jesus the death penalty the populace would rise at him. If he acquitted Him, the priests would be at odds with one of their own. Better yet, Herod was in Jerusalem for Passover and so could receive the prisoner at once.

The priests stood openmouthed but could do nothing except race ahead of the soldiers to the Hasmonean palace used by Herod while in Jerusalem. Herod received the news with great joy. Jesus the miracle-worker was coming to stand trial before him. He understood what Pilate was seeking to do and accepted it. From that day they were friends.

Herod couldn't have cared less about Caiaphas. He knew that thousands of Galileans followed

Jesus and owned Him as Messiah. He also knew that none of his spies had reported anything dangerous from the harmless Nazarene. He was not about to anger his subjects by condemning Him over some obscure temple violation. He had decided it would be an interesting diversion. He would question Jesus and ask Him to perform some of His magic. He had heard He had raised the dead.

He had an eagerness to see Jesus that bordered on an obsession of remorse. Herod had beheaded John the Baptist and had never rested well since. At one time he was convinced that Jesus was John risen from the dead. Now he eagerly awaited the interview.

Herod received the prisoner, along with the priests, into the gorgeous palace. He asked Him questions of the miracles he had heard ascribed to Him. Jesus looked gently back and said nothing. Herod leaned forward in his chair. Would this wonder-worker not perform a few signs, a miracle or two to prove His claims? Jesus remained silent.

The priests and elders recited all His crimes, but Herod was not interested in the ravings of the priests. He wanted some action from this so-called Messiah. But He was answering not a word. Didn't He know the power of Herod, king of Judea?

Herod looked contemptuously at Jesus. A king! Pah! He mocked Him. Tired, haggard through standing all night as well as being beaten, Jesus now sagged, trembling with weakness. A king in a filthy robe and a swollen bloody face. Herod laughed in His face and encouraged his soldiers to do the same. Then he called a servant who went

and quickly returned with a gorgeous robe. Herod
took it and swung it around Jesus' shoulders. A
robe for a king! Even Caiaphas laughed at the
ridiculous sight—a king that looked like a clown.
Herod dismissed them and told them to take Jesus
back to Pilate.

In the early morning sun they marched the man
called Messiah back to the Tower of Antonia.
Caiaphas was desperate. If he could not arrange
the death of Jesus within hours, all was lost. The
mob must scream for blood. If Pilate wouldn't give
the case, then they would give him a riot. That
would change his mind.

> And Pilate summoned the chief priests
> and the rulers and the people,
> and said to them, "You brought this man
> to me as one who incites the people to
> rebellion, and behold, having examined Him
> before you, I have found no guilt in this man
> regarding the charges which you make
> against Him.
> "No, nor has Herod, for he sent Him
> back to us; and behold, nothing deserving
> death has been done by Him.
> I will therefore punish Him and release
> Him."
>
> Luke 23:13-16

The crowd was murmuring angrily. Pilate
realized he would have a mob scene on his hands.
He was losing ground, having already made a fool
of himself. He had acquitted Jesus as not guilty.
He had then changed his mind and sent Him to the
Jewish king, who had returned Him dressed like a

clown not worthy of putting to trial. Now the justice of Rome had acquitted a second time and was hesitating before the angry threatening crowd.

It was the custom at Passover to release a prisoner, and Pilate saw it as the final out. He would give them the choice: a well-known political murderer called Barabbas—or Jesus, the one called Messiah.

The people's response threw him. They screamed, "Not this Man, but Barabbas" (John 18:40).

Shaking his head, Pilate knew he had lost control. Puzzled, he asked, "What then shall I do with Jesus who is called Christ?"

They all said, "Let Him be crucified!"

And he said, "Why, what evil has He done?"

But they kept shouting all the more, saying, "Let Him be crucified!" (see Matthew 27:22-23).

Turning to the soldiers guarding Jesus, he ordered Him to be scourged in a courtyard within the tower. The whole garrison came to see the show. Scourged Messiah! What a joke. The wicked pieces of bone and iron chain at the ends of the whip embraced His body, tearing His flesh into ribbons. Again and again the leather thongs lay on His body, ripping the skin until He was a mass of quivering raw pulp. Pilate ordered them to stop before He died. They untied Him and threw cold water over His limp body to revive Him. Every raw nerve screamed with pain as He returned to consciousness.

The soldiers received His sagging body into the barracks. Before they returned Him to the crowd, they would show Him what they thought of His claims to be king. One put a purple robe around

Him, while another took a crown made out of branches covered with vicious thorns and dug it into His head. Yet another took a stick and put it in His hand for a scepter. *The clown king of the Jews.* The king who thought He had a kingdom. What had He said, "My kingdom is not of this world?"

They came and knelt before Him in mock adoration: "Hail, King of the Jews!" (John 19:3). Then, rising, they spat in His face, laughing Him to scorn. One grabbed the mock scepter and beat Him on His swollen, bleeding cheeks. Jesus never said a word.

Pilate went out to face the priests and the mob: "Behold, I am bringing Him out to you, that you may know that I find no guilt in Him" (John 19:4).

Jesus was brought out by the soldiers who held Him. He was hardly recognizable. His face was swollen from the beating, and much of His beard had been ripped from His skin. With a magnificent flourish of his hand, Pilate said to the priests, "Behold, the Man!" (John 19:5).

He was playing for their pity, believing the sight of incredible suffering would satisfy them. To his amazement they screamed back, "Crucify, crucify!" (John 19:6).

Thoroughly shaken and confused, Pilate snapped, "Take Him yourselves, and crucify Him" (John 19:6). They couldn't. He knew they had to have his signature, and they knew it only too well.

The Jews answered him, "We have a law, and by that law He ought to die because He made Himself out to be the Son of God" (John 19:7).

Pilate moved from confusion to fear. Who was this Galilean? Dry-mouthed, he marched back up the steps into the Praetorium, and the soldiers brought Jesus to him. "Where are You from?" he asked (John 19:9). The question spoke to more than His birthplace. It almost reached out to ask if He really was God. Jesus did not answer.

Pilate was curious, that was all. He would never understand if he was told that this One was from everlasting. Before Rome was, He was the I AM. Pilate could never know that when Rome was dust, millions would worship this One.

Didn't this Nazarene want to be saved? Why didn't He show some cooperation? "You do not speak to me? Do You not know that I have authority to release You, and I have authority to crucify You?" (John 19:10).

With great difficulty Jesus spoke. His cracked lips were horribly swollen and His mouth dry tasting of blood. It was an effort to breathe, let alone speak: "You would have no authority over Me, unless it had been given you from above; for this reason he who delivered Me up to you has the greater sin" (John 19:11).

When Pilate stood again before the desperate, furious mob whipped to a frenzy by the priests, Caiaphas knew he had won. He had his fish, it was only a matter of reeling him in. It would be checkmate within minutes. It was a frightened man who slowly came down the steps. He obviously wanted to free Jesus but was cracking under the pressure of the mob.

The priests shouted their clinching words, "If you release this Man, you are no friend of Caesar; every one who makes himself out to be a king opposes Caesar" (John 19:12).

It was blackmail. Caiaphas was saying that unless Jesus was crucified today he would report the whole matter to Emperor Tiberius. Pilate found himself saying, "Behold, your King!" (John 19:14).

The answer came like a roar from the crowd, "Away with Him, away with Him, crucify Him!" (John 19:15).

Shouting now, trying to be heard above the frenzied screams, Pilate asked them, "Shall I crucify your King?" (John 19:15).

The priests led the chant, leaning into the hated Gentile's residence, spitting the words into the confused governor's face, "We have no king but Caesar" (John 19:15).

Every Jew chanting would have stabbed any Roman in the back and joined a revolt against Rome if he thought they had half a chance. Now they sounded more devoted to Caesar than Pilate himself. They preferred slavery to Rome rather than the kingdom the young Messiah offered.

The priests had won. Declaring himself innocent of the blood of this man, Pilate delivered Him to be crucified. The elated mob thundered, "His blood be on us and on our children!" (Matthew 27:25).

19

On a Hill Far Away

Suddenly, Pilate determined to have the last word and sum up in a sentence what he knew inside of him but could not articulate. In crucifixion the name and crime of the victim were nailed above his head. He called the centurion and ordered that the crime of this man be written in Hebrew, Latin, and Greek. It was to read "JESUS THE NAZARENE, THE KING OF THE JEWS" (John 19:19). Pilate had never heard of *Shiloh,* a king from whom all others found their meaning. All he knew was that if the Jews ever had a king, he had just ordered His crucifixion.

A procession of cavalry formed at the tower. In the center a rectangle of foot soldiers formed a cell of spears around three men—Jesus, who was to be crucified in place of Barabbas, and two thieves. In front of each person were three soldiers, one carrying the board declaring the crime of the man about to be executed.

The place of execution was called Golgotha, or the Skull; some called it Calvary. The crosspiece was a roughly fashioned three-inch by five-inch timber about six feet long. A hole in the center would snugly receive the top of the upright when they got to the Skull.

Only as the procession began to move away from the Roman fort, with Jesus staggering between the prison of spears, did Caiaphas begin to relax. He preened himself. He had saved the Lord's nation from abandoning the temple and had silenced this blaspheming peasant who had spoken His vile words before the Lord God. It was a good day for Israel, and he had fulfilled his office of high priest well.

The road to Golgotha was lined with people. The place itself was a crossroads, and pilgrims poured in from all corners for Passover, anxious to be settled before the Sabbath. They jostled on the narrow street, generally silent except for a cry of pity for the prisoners and anger at Rome.

Then Jesus fell. He had been staggering all of the way and the load suddenly became too heavy. Lurching forward, the crossbar went from His hands, and He crumbled into the dust. The crown of thorns bit deeply into His head, causing fresh blood to ooze over the caked streaks already on His head and face.

To order this wreck of a man to pick up the cross would have caused a riot from the crowd. Knowing this, the centurion scanned the mob irritably. A dark muscular man stood out; he was obviously a pilgrim. The Roman ordered him to pick up the fallen crosspiece and carry it for the prisoner. He was Simon from Cyrene.

Free from the torturous burden of the cross-piece, Jesus staggered and reeled between the box of spears toward Golgotha. The execution spot was a rocky hill some fifteen feet high at the meeting of two roads. Behind the hill was a garden and in it an unused tomb that belonged to Joseph of Arimathea. Starkly silhouetted against the azure sky were the uprights over which the crosspieces would fit.

Some of the crowd had followed to see the end—among them were Caiaphas and the chief priests. A handful of weeping women pressed close to the cross. They were the immediate followers of Jesus—Mary, His mother; Mary Magdalene; and Salome, mother of James and John. Young John was there, too, but the absence of all the other male disciples was a sad commentary on their brave words the previous night.

At the sight of the cross, one thief broke into oaths and curses at the Roman government and at God. Jesus looked almost thankful. For this He had chosen to be born, and toward this very hour every hour of His life had moved. Simon dumped the crosspiece down and stared at Jesus. He never forgot the person he saw.

The prisoners were stripped and their clothes put aside to be divided among the soldiers who would guard the crosses. The arms were then laid back to the crossbar fitted under the necks of the victims. Five-inch nails were driven through the hollow spot in Jesus' wrist at the base of the hand, securely attaching Him to the bar.

When they had done this to Jesus, two soldiers took either end of the crosspiece, lifted and dragged Him up the ladders to the upright. Finding the hole, they let the bar drop with a sickening thud over the upright, jarring every bone in His body.

The board bearing His name and crime was nailed into place where the upright and the crosspiece met, serving the double purpose of displaying the crime and securing the two pieces of wood. All of this time the full weight of His body hung on His wrists. Now His legs were pushed up, the right foot placed over the left and nailed together to the cross.

Crucifixion was the most sophisticated in-strument of torture and death devised by man. Exhausted from prior beatings and the pain of the position he was nailed in, the victim would be forced to hang forward on the nails through his wrists. The rest would bring into play a new set of agonies. Apart from the muscle spasms in the shoulders and arms, the muscles at the side of the chest paralyzed, making exhalation impossible. In order to breathe, the victim would be forced to raise himself by pushing down on the nail through the feet. He would be able to breathe only until the pain in the feet and legs became unbearable, forcing him to lower himself to his hanging position. This grotesque exercise went on until the wretched creature could raise himself no more and slowly suffocated.   Caiaphas and his chief priests, along with elders from the Sanhedrin, stared at the bloody, naked, writhing humanity. The high priest's face was contorted with rage. Coming as close to the cross as the guard would allow, he screamed, "He saved others; He cannot save Himself. He is the King of Israel; let Him now come down from the cross, and we shall believe in Him. HE TRUSTS IN

GOD; LET HIM DELIVER HIM NOW, IF HE TAKES PLEASURE IN HIM; for He said, 'I am the Son of God' " (Matthew 27:42-43).

So much attention was on Him that one of the soldiers came over and studied Him as He gasped for breath. The sign sat above His head. *What a throne! What a king!* He sneered in His face: "And the soldiers also mocked Him, coming up to Him, offering Him sour wine, and saying, 'If You are King of the Jews, save Yourself!'" (Luke 23:36-37).

It was twelve noon and the sun had been climbing into its full heat. Someone noticed that it was beginning to get dark. The sun was shining but the earth was shrouded as by a heavy veil.

The soldiers gambled incessantly, the sound of the dice clicking on the smooth rock. The possessions of the three men were divided evenly among them. One item was left over, the tunic of Jesus. It was an expensive garment woven without seams. The dice rolled again on the Skull rock, and one half-drunken soldier grabbed the bloodstained garment and stuffed it among his things.

It was nearly the end for Jesus. The effort to lift Himself was becoming harder. It had never been easy. The noise of the rolling dice, the raucous laughter and shouts of the man who had won His garment, all floated up to Him as from a great distance. They were the men who sadistically had nailed Him where He was. The face of Caiaphas leered at Him through the gloom and then faded in a green mist as Jesus struggled for consciousness. Caiaphas wouldn't leave until the end. Like a vulture, he waited for death. The face of Pilate, weak, torn in indecision, drifted before Him, then the soldiers spitting, punching, laughing in the barracks room. The man who had delighting in laying the whip across Him, seemed momentarily to stand before Him and laugh.

Not far away, Judas, who walked with Him closer than thousands, now swung in a wide arc by his neck from a tree—dead by his own hand. The crowd came back into focus. It wasn't the presence of the priests that hurt, but the absence of the disciples who should have been there. Last night they had vowed to die for Him. It was the focal point of weak men and all hell. Surveying them all, He lifted Himself and cried out, "Father, forgive them; for they do not know what they are doing" (Luke 23:34).

The thief who already had violently cursed, twisted his neck and tried to look at Jesus: "Are You not the Christ? Save Yourself and us!" (Luke 23:39).

The other thief had said nothing until now. Raising himself, he tried to look at his blaspheming companion: "Do you not even fear God, since you are under the same sentence of condemnation? And we indeed justly, for we are receiving what we deserve for our deeds; but this man has done nothing wrong." And he was saying, "Jesus, remember me when You come in Your kingdom!" (Luke 23:40-42).

Jesus turned to him—the only one in that scene of blood, wretchedness, and despair who could see that there was a kingdom beyond the cross. The men who had heard Him speak of a return after going away and a glorious kingdom set up upon that return had all fled, believing that this was the end. Yet a thief could see that the king was on the cross and a kingdom was being established. Jesus said, "Truly I say to you, today you shall be with Me in Paradise" (Luke 23:43).

The last minutes were approaching and He cried out, "MY GOD, MY GOD, WHY HAST THOU FORSAKEN ME?" (Matthew 27:46). It was the first line of a psalm David had written one thousand years before, in which he had described this moment as if he had been the victim on the cross (see Psalms 22). This was the hour He had faced in Gethsemane when, human sin laid upon Him, He had known the presence of His Father in wrath against it: the sense of being deserted of love and the light of fellowship. It was out of a darkness deeper than the eerie darkness covering the land, the darkness of death, that He had cried those words.

A few moments later He gasped out the words "I am thirsty" (John 19:28). A soldier came and stared at the man about to expire. Taking a sponge, he dipped it in a jar of sour wine and pushed it on a branch to His lips.

Pulling Himself up again, Jesus said, "FATHER, INTO THY HANDS I COMMIT MY SPIRIT" (Luke 23:46). He was releasing His spirit. No man took His life from Him; He chose to lay it down.

Then His last words. The cry was loud. Too loud for a man in His condition. Everyone heard and turned in amazement: "It is finished!" (John 19:30). It was not a sob of despair, but the loud triumphant cry of One who has accomplished a mission.

The Romans looked up. It reminded them of the call of a general who had just seen the decisive turn in the battle. The victor's cry. John heard and vividly remembered His words as they had followed Him into Gethsemane: "Take courage; I have overcome the world" (John 16:33).

The earth trembled, cracks appeared. "Earth-quake!" shouted a soldier and leaped to his feet. The priests in

199

the temple felt the wrenching of the earth and were transfixed in horror as the veil separating the holy of holies was suddenly ripped from top to bottom with an awful sound. They didn't know that the way into the holiest was now open and a new covenant was now in effect.

The Sabbath was coming on and the priests insisted that the dead be removed by that time. The prisoners must die—quickly. The way Rome hastened the death was to break the legs of the crucified. Unable to lift themselves up, they were dead within a few minutes as paralysis set into their chests.

They came to break the legs of Jesus and were amazed to find Him dead already. One of the soldiers could not pass up one last act of sadism. He stood back and ran his spear into His heart. Blood and a water substance came out. But they didn't break any bones.

John stood, his mind numb. *He was the resurrection and the life—the Messiah of Israel. How could He die?*

20

No Greater Love

Jesus died according to the purpose of God, and by His own choice. He willingly embraced that purpose. Death was the reason He had chosen to be born, and His choosing to die was the ultimate obedience to which He was called. It was this divine will that His shuddering human will had accepted in Gethsemane.

The disciples had heard Him speak of the shameful death that He would have to accomplish in Jerusalem. But they had not truly heard Him. They had heard the prophets proclaiming Messiah's kingdom of righteousness and a new covenant in which sin and iniquity would be remembered no more. A kingdom in which God's holy law would be established forever. A kingdom of righteousness, in which sin was put away by God, would have to be founded on a blood sacrifice that would end all sacrifices. From the beginning, the approach of sinful man to God the holy One was always understood to be through the shedding of blood: "For the life of the flesh is in the blood, and I have given it to you on the altar to make atonement for your souls; for it is the blood by reason of the life that makes atonement" (Leviticus 17:11).

The blood sacrifice was for God before it was for man. Man had mocked His holiness by sin. Any kingdom wherein God and man fellowshiped had to be founded on the absolute rightness of God's law. Sin must be punished or God would be less than God.

God is committed, by the necessity of His being, to punish sin. He is also eternal love reaching out to rebellious man. *His love could not receive man unless sin was punished, and so He chose to bear the punishment Himself.* In this way God established the necessity of His holiness and received man at the same time.

His holy wrath is not a vindictive action but rather the necessary vindication of His holiness. Because of this, He gave animal sacrifices that were substitutes for sinners. Bearing man's sin, they took the death that belonged to the sinner until the day God came Himself, the final offering.

When the worshiper took the animal sacrifice in his hand, he was accepting God's prior act, His holy solution to man's sin. The first act in the offering was for the worshiper to lay his hands on the animal, confessing God's holiness and his own guilt that had so justly incurred the wrath of the holy One. In that confession, his polluted life became one with the flawless lifeblood of the animal. The animal became as the worshiper. Its history would henceforth be the history of the man. Whatever now happened to the life of the beast happened by God's gift to the man.

What was it that God demanded of man that he could give via the substitute animal? It was not blood—as blood—that meant anything to God. God is spirit and could never be satisfied with material blood.

The Creator demanded of His creation total, trusting, obedience—an obedience that was in its very nature a willing, chosen death to self-will, the hallmark of the original lie. He was called upon to offer up the whole self for the doing of God's will. In the pouring out of the substitute animal's blood in death, the offerer saw his very self poured out as an oblation to God to do His final will.

But the first demand of God's will was that sin should be punished, and the wages of sin was death. The guilt of the worshiper had been transferred to the flawless animal. The release of its lifeblood submitted to the will of God's wrath allowed the sins to be covered. The wages of sin had been temporarily covered as the substitute in death was absolved of the guilt it carried.

The shed blood, still the substitute for the offerer, was cleansed of the guilt it bore. The priest took it to the altar, where it was sprinkled, symbolizing that through his substitute the offerer may come and fellowship with the holy One.

But the life of an animal poured out could never adequately deal with sin. Man was a moral agent. How could an amoral beast take his place? The heart of the sacrificial act was lacking in the beast. The man may have chosen to accept the animal as God's substitute, *but the sacrifice could not choose to be that substitute.* If it had been a moral being it would be the height of immorality to place the guilt of another on an unwilling substitute.

Man must have a sacrifice that is at least equal, but himself sinless, *and willing*—a substitute that satisfies not only man, but God, whose holiness is being vindicated.

Only God can satisfy God, and only the holy answer the holy. The animals were only shadows finding their substance in the prior will of God. They were scale models of the then yet future coming of God into human history after their constant bloody flow had etched His holy demands and purposes into the race. The Messiah would be that perfect offering that finally dealt with sin and ushered in the kingdom of God's righteousness. A few hours before, Jesus had told His disciples that the new covenant had arrived *in His blood.*

In this One designated the Lamb of God, is the act of free choice that no offering before had been capable of. As He waited for the men who came to arrest Him, it was with the regal calmness of an act accomplished, a path deliberately chosen. That act was summed in the words of His prayer, "Not My will but Thine be done." This was the total giving of self to God that had been demanded of men by the holy One since the expulsion from Eden. The Messiah made not the greatest self-sacrifice, but rather the final sacrifice *of self.*

It was *this act* that was presented to the Father from Messiah. He was man, but He was man who willed as God. It was God responding to God's demands, but God was in the form of man who therefore included all men in His act. In that act of deliberate choice, His blood had begun to be shed—for the life is in the blood. When He chose in Gethsemane to accept the will of the Father even to death, it was the complete and vital obedience of the holy to the holy.

In this real man the act was the active death of His holy self-will into the holy will of God. He *willed* such a surrender of self. He did not merely resign to it, nor was He simply a volunteer. The choice was deliberately made in love for the Father and holiness. He was to be the sin offering, but His free choice made it into a thank offering.

The events from Gethsemane to Skull Hill were not so much God's accepting sacrifice but rather His *making* it. It was God who, in His choice to die for men, made the first sacrifice before time. All of man's sacrifices were but responses to that. Now the decision is actual in history, and God carries His sacrifice to the extreme.

The bearers of God's sword of justice were not forced into their role of executors, helplessly predestined to do as they did. In Jesus Messiah they faced God's holiness. *Every part of their being hated holiness.* Their hatred was used of God against His Son, but they were morally responsible for their atrocities.

As He faced this hour, Jesus had recognized it as a conflict with *Satan,* the master these men had chosen. He overcame by accepting the men, Satan, and death itself from the hand of His Father as His judgment against sin.

The act of being lifted up by the God-ordained justice to hang on a tree was understood by the

Law as being cursed by God. The action of the judge was seen as God's act of Judgment: "CURSED IS EVERY ONE WHO HANGS ON A TREE" (Galatians 3:13).

When Roman justice saw fit to nail Him to a cross, Jesus accepted it as the divine curse, the sum total of God's antagonism to sin laid upon Him. He accepted it as right and glorified holiness that was stating that so essential is holiness that the God-man must die rather then let sin go unpunished.

In being made sin for us, the God-man experienced sin both as man and as God. He felt its deadly malignancy and the unspeakable horror of sin to the holy being of God. He knew that the holy One and sin could not coexist. *It must be removed, even though it would demand of Him the extreme penalty.* Feeling the pain of sin as only God can, He felt the judgment of sin as only man could.

His sufferings and death as man were the placing of His whole self beside man under the wrath of God, declaring that God was right in His judgment. It was this, the very essence of death, that He shrank from in Gethsemane. He knew that He was to be the substitute, to be treated as the all-inclusive sinner of history. The Father looked upon Him in those hours as though He was all the sinners of the world rolled into one.

On the cross, His sufferings came to this indescribable head. The darkness that shrouded creation was but an outward shadow of the inward experience of the all-inclusive man. Out of that darkness came the most hideous cry ever to fall on human ears: "My God, My God, why hast Thou forsaken Me?"

Jesus was not mistaken in His cry, but accurately describing His sufferings that went far beyond the recordable sufferings of His body. The prophets had glimpsed the meeting of sin in Him. During those hours He was the focus of the sin of the world. "For my iniquities are gone over my head; As a heavy burden they weigh too much for me" (Psalms 38:4).

"For evils beyond number have surrounded me; My iniquities have overtaken me, so that I am not able to see; They are more numerous than the hairs of my head; And my heart has failed me" (Psalms 40:12).

The most horrific suffering was not received directly from man, but from God:

> Surely our griefs He Himself bore,
> And our sorrows He carried;
> Yet we ourselves esteemed Him stricken,
> Smitten of God, and afflicted.
> But He was pierced through for our transgressions,
> He was crushed for our iniquities;
> The chastening for our well-being fell upon Him,
> And by His scourging we are healed.
> All of us like sheep have gone astray,
> Each of us has turned to his own way;
> But the Lord has caused the iniquity of us all
> To fall on Him.
>
> Isaiah 53:4-6

> But the Lord was pleased
> To crush Him, putting Him to grief.
> Isaiah 53:10

The wrath of God against sin fell directly on Him, man's substitute. As man's substitute, He felt that antagonism of God against sin as a lost soul in hell would feel it:

> Thou has put me in the lowest pit,
> In dark places, in the depths.
> Thy wrath has rested upon me,
> And Thou hast afflicted me with all Thy
> waves.
> Psalms 88:6-7

> I suffer Thy terrors; I am overcome.
> Thy burning anger has passed over me;
> Thy terrors have destroyed me.
> Psalms 88:15-16

Gone was the sense of the Father's support, and the awareness of the Father's love. It was not only a matter of losing the joy of communion with the Father, but in its place was the active awareness of the Father's wrath toward Him as the sin bearer for the race. His sufferings exceeded the aggregate sufferings of the race, for He was the infinite person whose value outweighed that of all other men combined.

Such a pouring out of life to the Father was enough. Man, in this man, was taken to judgment and justly punished. God's holiness was glorified. Having done all, Jesus embraced the final wages of sin in His body and shouted, "It is finished."

Nicodemus had openly joined with Joseph of Arimathea in asking Pilate for the body of Jesus. The Sabbath was almost upon them and the burial had to be hurried. If it could be arranged, more spices would be added after the Sabbath was over. Until such a time, the most basic procedure was followed—the body was wrapped in yards of linen interlined with spices and gums.

Joseph lay the body in his tomb and a great stone was rolled over the entrance.

> His grave was assigned to be with wicked men,
> Yet with a rich man in His death;
> Although He had done no violence,
> Nor was there any deceit in His mouth.
>
> Isaiah 53:9

21

"He Is Not Here"

The disciples were grief-stricken. John accounted to them of the tragic events he had witnessed at Golgotha. Their paralyzed minds tried to take in that their life and hope was gone. With Him, their dreams of His kingdom lay dead, bound in sticky spices in a tomb under Skull Hill.

Back in Jerusalem, Caiaphas had a problem. When Pilate had ordered the crucifixion, the body of the prisoner became the property of Rome to be thrown into a common grave and guarded by Roman soldiers. Now two members of the Sanhedrin had received the body and buried it in a private grave. It meant that the body was no longer Rome's responsibility to guard. Today was the Sabbath, but tomorrow anything could happen. Caiaphas shuddered. *If His followers came, stole the body, spread a tale of miracles* . . . his thoughts trailed away. Bad enough error that the rabble had believed Him to be Messiah, he dare not think of where it would end if they thought He would rise again. He had to get a Roman guard to secure the grave against the possibility of a worse heresy.

The chief priests and elders decided to return again to the Roman. They stood eyeing the governor with triumph as he glared at them with unashamed hate. "Sir, we remember that when He was still alive that deceiver said, 'After three days I am to rise again.' Therefore, give orders for the grave to be made secure until the third day, lest the disciples come and steal Him away and say to the people, "He has risen from the dead" (Matthew 27:63-64).

Pilate snarled out his reply. They were getting no Roman guard; let them use their own temple guard: "You have a guard; go, make it as secure as you know how" (Matthew 27:65).

This is what Caiaphas had dreaded. If a riot broke out or if the body was stolen, the temple was to blame. All Rome supplied was an official seal across the stone.

The guards took up their position by the end of the Sabbath. They sat and then investigated the perimeter of the garden on the hours. The night was still, broken only by raucous laughs as they exchanged jokes.

It was early morning and everything was still in deep darkness. The guards wished for the first light, when they could be replaced. Suddenly the earth buckled and rolled with an earthquake, and the garden was lit by a radiance of light that was as bright as lightning. In the middle of the radiance was a man who was himself the source of the light. He rolled the stone away. It would take ten strong men to roll that great stone with the ease he did. They heard it grind, rock against rock.

The earthquake had thrown their balance and the light before them struck a terror into them. Their limbs would not obey them; they were as dead men, beholding some awesome spectacle. The grave they were guarding was now empty and Jehovah's angel was in the garden, now sitting on the great stone, the Roman seal hanging pathetically on the ground. Their strength began to return and to a man they rose and fled into the city to the house of Caiaphas.

As they ran in blind terror, a handful of women led by Mary Magdalene came through the unlit streets of the lower city toward the garden of Joseph. They carried the spices to complete the burial ritual left over from the day before the Sabbath.

Caiaphas listened to the frightened guards, his lips in a tight line. The worst had happened. For a fleeting second the thought presented itself that this man could be who He claimed to be, but was dismissed at once. What had happened he was not quite sure. Certainly it was very real, whatever it was. He looked in disgust at the whimpering men that stood in front of him in the grey light of dawn. Whatever it was that had taken place in the garden of Joseph, the peasants from Galilee must be shielded from any suggestion that He had risen.

The women came through the city gates, talking in low tones. They had come at this early hour at the instigation of Mary Magdalene. There was Mary; Cleopas; Salome, wife of Zebedee and mother of James and John; and Joanna. They had not even wakened the men folk, but had quietly left the house in an unthinking enthusiasm. Now it dawned on them. Who would move the stone so that they could complete the burial details? In their grief and desire to administer the last loving care to the body, it had not even occurred to them.

If it had been lighter, and they less intent, they would have noticed the grass and flowers trampled by the departed guards. What they did see was the stone rolled away from the entrance.

They hesitated and drew closer together. Cautiously, they advanced toward the black hole of the tomb set against the grey of the dawn. They were afraid of the eerie world of the dead and stopped at the door.

Then they saw him. A shadowy figure in white sitting on the ledge where the body had lain. Terror gripped them and as one person they turned and fled. The young man called after them, perplexity in his voice:

> "Do not be afraid; for I know that you are looking for Jesus who has been crucified.
>
> "He is not here, for He has risen, just as He said. Come, see the place where He was lying.
>
> "And go quickly and tell His disciples that He has risen from the dead; and behold, He is going before you into Galilee, there you will see Him; behold, I have told you."
>
> Matthew 28:5-7

The words almost arrested them. *Risen from the dead.* Against reason, they believed somewhere within them and their joy began to rise even as their heads told them that some persons had stolen the body. They fled through the rays of the rising sun to blurt out the news to the men. Mary Magdalene went on ahead and was soon breathlessly pounding on the door where Peter was sleeping. The words came in gasps, "They have taken away the Lord out of the tomb, and we do not know where they have laid Him" (John 20:2).

Peter stopped only to grab a coat against the chill of early morning. Young John was awake and came running. In his excitement he outran Peter and got to the tomb first, but he stayed outside while Peter entered it. Then he went in. They took in the scene. What they saw convinced them that they were not witnessing a grave robbery. They were beholding something infinitely beyond a grave desecration. Lying where the body of Jesus had been was the stiff cocoon, slightly depressed, that had housed the body. In a separate place was the turban that had been around His head. *But the body was gone.*

Any human stealing the body would have ripped off the grave clothes or taken them with the body. No, it wasn't robbery—perhaps it was resurrection! The body had gone, leaving the wrappings in place. Faith tried to stir in their hearts, but they were at a loss to explain what they saw. They wanted to believe, but somehow could not, "For as yet they did not know the Scripture, that He must rise again from the dead" (John 20:9, NKJV). They walked slowly back to the city to tell the others.

Mary Magdalene stayed. She was weeping at the entrance to the tomb when through her tears she saw two men sitting at either end of the hollow of grave clothes. One of these was the white-clothed being who had frightened her an hour before. The two of them looked puzzled. How come the mortal did not understand? "And they said to her, 'Woman, why are you weeping?' " (John 20:13).

She remembered it all later. Now she neither understood nor cared to answer. It was then that she heard the sound behind her. Turning around, she saw a figure silhouetted against the bright morning. The person looked somewhat familiar but she did not recognize who it was.

Supposing Him to be the gardener, she blurted out the words, "Sir, if you have carried Him away, tell me where you have laid Him, and I will take Him away" (John 20:15).

215

The voice that answered her could never be mistaken: *"Mary!"* She knew with an understanding that defied her intellect that this was Jesus Messiah indeed.

She shouted through her tears, "Rabboni!" (which means, *Teacher*) (John 20:16, author's italics). She clawed at Him, clinging to His robes.

He gently released her grasp and said, "Stop clinging to Me; for I have not yet ascended to the Father; but go to My brethren, and say to them, 'I ascend to My Father and your Father, and My God and your God'" (John 20:17).

Caiaphas had heard the story of the soldiers for what seemed to be the hundredth time. The elders carefully instructed the soldiers what to do: "You are to say, 'His disciples came by night and stole Him away while we were asleep' " (Matthew 28:13).

If they had been Roman soldiers, such a confession would have meant immediate execution. However, the Roman seal could bring Rome into it and bring further trouble. Caiaphas assured the men it would be explained to the governor if ever he heard of it. A fat purse was handed to each soldier and they went, puzzled, into the morning to tell their story and earn their bribe.

Caiaphas stood thoughtfully among the dispersing elders. Stroking his beard, he uneasily wondered if they had heard the last of the tomb that now gaped empty a few thousand feet from where they had bribed the soldiers. If they *had* stolen the body it should be a simple matter to find it and expose the fraud. The high priest moved awkwardly across the room. *Somehow He knew he would never find the body.*

22

Resurrection and Revelation

Jesus could not die unless He chose to; He was sinless, the holy One, and death has no power over the holy. Death came in with sin. Life belongs to the holy as naturally as death belongs to sin. In order to die, Jesus had to willingly lay His life down, which He did when He assumed the sins of the world. *He could therefore be held by death only so long as He bore the sin of man.*

It was in that strong hope He had cried, "It is finished." He had yet to embrace death in His body when He shouted that, but He saw through the darkness and the horror and shame of the grave. Death could not hold Him. It held Him only so long as the sin of others met in *Him.* In that faith, He committed His spirit to the Father, expecting resurrection. The psalmist had seen this and spoken of the Messiah's assurance: "For Thou wilt not abandon my soul to Sheol; Neither wilt Thou allow Thy Holy One to see the pit. Thou wilt make known to me the path of life" (Psalms 16:10-11).

The Resurrection was a twofold declaration. It stated that the sin that took Him to death had been put away, and that He *was* the holy One and could not be held in death. They had cried, "If You are the Son of God, come down from the cross." It was by staying on the cross and being raised from the dead that He proved forever He was the Son of God.

This meant the kingdom of Satan was des-troyed. The authority of Satan, his right to be called the prince of this age, was that man believed his lie. Man's rebellion made him legal prey of the rebel. The guilt before God that all members of the kingdom of darkness shared was the badge of Satan's prisoners.

When Jesus took man's place, He entered that darkness and felt the authority of Satan over man. In the substitute, Satan had all men. To have kept Him in death would be to have won forever. But the poured-out lifeblood was enough. God's holiness was satisfied, and man could be justified without violating that holiness. The Resurrection was the declaration of God to the universe of men, angels, and devils, and primarily to Himself, that He could bring sinner man to Himself and *glorify* His holiness.

In that Resurrection the first words of hope man had heard were fulfilled:

> And the Lord God said to the serpent: . . .
> "And I will put enmity
> Between you and the woman,
> And between your seed and her seed;

He shall bruise you on the head,
And you shall bruise him on the heel."
Genesis 3:14-15

On the cross on Calvary, a man—seed of the woman, the all-inclusive man—had *as* man and *for* man broken the head of the serpent beneath His feet: "Inasmuch then as the children have partaken of flesh and blood, He Himself likewise shared in the same, that through death He might destroy him who had the power of death, that is, the devil, and release those who through fear of death were all their lifetime subject to bondage" (Hebrews 2:14-15, NKJV). He had done what he had been manifested to do: "destroy the works of the devil' (1 John 3:8)

The cross, from one point of view, was the helplessness of God, yet that was His triumph over man's great enemy. It was the humiliation and shame of God, but *that* was His glory forever. Nailed to a cross was the preparation for the victory procession. Paul spoke of God's power, "which He brought about in Christ, when He raised Him from the dead, and seated Him at His right hand in the heavenly places, far above all rule and authority and power and dominion, and every name that is named, not only in this age, but also in the one to come. And He put all things in subjection under His feet" (Ephesians 1:20-22).

But Jesus had come to do more than release man from guilt and the power of Satan. He had come to bring man back to the throne he had lost, to reign as God's vice-regent over the earth and the universe. A reign in fellowship with God, joyously obeying and worshiping Him.

It was of this that He had spoken so urgently to the men in the upper room. He was going to prepare a place of their dwelling in God and God in them. Men on earth united with God. The task Messiah had been sent to accomplish was not only to put sin away, but to bring man to God—to an active, functioning fellowship with Deity.

The new covenant not only assured that sin would be remembered no more, but promised that men would *know* the Lord. The expression "know" to the Hebrew was speaking of a fellowship as in marriage, a transparent knowing of love. To this man was called, to enter into a transparent love relationship with God once his sin had been dealt with.

Jesus as man and for man died, was buried, and rose from the dead. Now as man and for man He will go into the glory of God's uncovered holiness, the first one of millions who will follow through Him to live eternally in union with God.

So outside the empty tomb He spoke to Mary of a new relationship established. He spoke of "My Father *and your Father.* " Because of His death and resurrection that relationship had been established for Mary and all others who would believe. Now He will ascend, receive the Spirit and bring that relationship to the experience of all on earth who would believe in Him.

As Mary ran back to despairing disciples, Jesus entered the invisible world of uncreated light. The invisible is the center of the visible and the source of all that happens in the visible. The visible universe is the effect; all causes are in the invisible. Whatever may appear to be in the visible world, ultimate reality is in the invisible.

Many years later John was given a vision of what happened in that invisible as Mary ran on her way. He records it in highly symbolic language that communicates a very real event in chapters 4 and 5 of Revelation. That which holds all John's attention as he enters the heavenly dimension is the throne of God. The physical world of man is not running disordered and meaninglessly. Life is not a madman's dream. The events of Golgotha are the center of the holy decrees that issue from the sovereign God who was all things according to His wise purpose.

He tries to describe the glory of God. It appeared like the radiant crystal of jasper, and the bloody red of sardius stone, all radiant and flashing before the eyes of John. The awful holiness of God, expressed to sinner man in fiery holiness, is the message from the throne. The throne has the sound of thunder and lightning in the vision, reminiscent of Sinai and the giving of the Law. The throne of God is established on His righteousness. He cannot deny Himself, He must rid His creation of evil.

How shall man be enabled to approach God? The rainbow around the throne is an echo of the covenant God made with Noah when He placed the bow in the clouds as the covenant seal that His judgment against man's sin would be held back by His mercy and that never again would He destroy all of humanity.

But John's attention is riveted to a scroll in God's right hand. Upon God's throne of sovereign rule He has His purpose for man. But man's sin has sealed the book (scroll). The question rang through the throne room, "Who is worthy to open the book and to break its seals?"

And no one in heaven, or on the earth, or under the earth, was able to open the book, or to look into it (Revelation 5:2-3).

At the news John wept greatly—but then one of the elders said to John, "Stop weeping—behold, the Lion that is from the tribe of Judah, the Root of David, has overcome so as to open the book and its seven seals" (Revelation 5:5).

The conqueror who has put off man's sin and trampled his enemies underfoot is announced with titles given Him that sum up all the prophets. He was Shiloh, the king that every Israelite king had anticipated, the Lion of Judah. If of Judah, then He was the seed of Abraham through whom all nations should be blessed. They call Him the Root of David, David's descendant who should reign over Israel forever. He has not only come, but now comes to claim His throne.

John turned to see the Lion come to claim His throne, the conqueror who had torn His enemies. Instead of a lion, he sees the glory of God's holiness, "a Lamb as it had been slain." The enemies of God were destroyed by the Lamb of God dying for them. He who was the king was also the Lamb of sacrifice who had glorified God's holiness.

He enters the awful glory of that throne and receives from God the right to bring to pass among men His purposes. No man had ever entered that presence before. They had approached only by mercy. The Man, who was the all-inclusive man, enters into the presence, not by mercy, but by the right of His own holiness.

The holy Man comes to the holy One and is accepted on His own merit. He carries in Him all men who would believe. In His merit, on the basis of His sacrifice for them, they too would be received into fellowship with Deity dreamed of only by prophets and seers. He had prepared a place in the glory of the Father's presence by His shed blood. Where He was, they would be also.

It was the coronation that all ages had strained toward. It was the beginning of a new age, a new day that the Lord had made in His holy wisdom. A kingdom had come into being where all subjects in the king were united with God forever.

Daniel had seen the coronation that John describes, calling the Lamb, the Son of Man:

> I kept looking in the night visions,
> And behold, with the clouds of heaven
> One like a Son of Man was coming,
> And He came up to the Ancient of Days
> And was presented before Him.
> And to Him was given dominion,
> Glory and a kingdom,
> That all the peoples, nations, and men of
> every language
> Might serve Him.
> His dominion is an everlasting dominion
> Which will not pass away;
> And His kingdom is one
> Which will not be destroyed.
>
> Daniel 7:13-14

The Messiah King sat on the throne in Zion, and what had been prophecy for a thousand years became history. In that day the Lord fulfilled all His promises to mankind, to Abraham, David, and Israel.

All heaven filled with praise. John heard all ages of men who would praise Him for carrying them by His blood to the Father. He heard angels adoring Him even though they themselves did not know His redemption. Even nature and brute beasts joined in adoring the Lamb, who through His death had lifted the curse from them:

> "Worthy art Thou . . . for Thou wast slain, and didst purchase for God with Thy blood men from every tribe and tongue and people and nation.
>
> "And Thou hast made them to be a kingdom and priests to our God; and they will reign upon the earth."
>
> And I looked, and I heard the voice of many angels around the throne and the living creatures and the elders; and the number of them was myriads of myriads, and thousands of thousands,
>
> saying with a loud voice,
>
> "Worthy is the Lamb that was slain to receive power and riches and wisdom and might and honor and glory and blessing."
>
> And every created thing which is in heaven and on the earth and under the earth and on the sea, and all things in them, I heard saying,
>
> "To Him who sits on the throne and to the Lamb, be blessing and honor and glory and dominion forever and ever."
>
> Revelation 5:9-13

Man in Jesus Messiah had been restored to rulership. In this One, man now ruled the universe, subduing it to the purposes of God. Rulership had passed into the hands of another Man, a second Adam, the beginner in Himself of a new race. By His death and resurrection He had established holiness forever in the earth. A kingdom was founded wherein God's law would be loved and pursued, for it would be written on the hearts of men. In that dominion of the Lamb, men would walk with heads held high, knowing that they had been declared righteous by the holy One. Here was the prince of the kings of the earth who ruled over all rulers to bring to pass His Father's purpose.

> Therefore also God highly exalted Him, and bestowed on Him the name which is above every name,
>
> that at the name of Jesus every knee should bow, of those who are in heaven, and on earth, and under the earth,
>
> and that every tongue should confess that Jesus Christ is Lord, to the glory of God the Father.
>
> Philippians 2:9-11

23

Where Now?

But how would men know of this cosmic achievement celebrated in the heavens? How would a sinner come to reign in a heavenly sphere with the Lamb? What would happen that could cause men to live on earth and yet be in a real kingdom that has a throne in heaven? How can heaven's glories, the true Mount Zion, be extended to earth and lived in by mortals who are yet in flesh?

In His coronation, Jesus Messiah was given the Holy Spirit to bestow on all those who would come under His rule. *In the giving of the Spirit, the glory of heaven would be brought into the world of men.*

The prophets had often seen the age of Messiah as being the activity of the Spirit. Isaiah looked at the desert dryness of Israel's spiritual life and saw it transformed into pasture and forest—life out of death *at the coming of the Spirit:*

> For I will pour out water on the thirsty
> land
> And streams on the dry ground;
> I will pour out My Spirit on your off-
> spring,
> And My blessing on your descendants;
> And they will spring up among the grass
> Like poplars by streams of water.
>
> Isaiah 44:3-4

This time of the springing up of life would bring to man the inner witness that he belonged to the Lord. No longer would an outward sign determine an Israelite, but the Spirit's presence: "This one will say, 'I am the Lord's' . . . And another will write on his hand, 'Belonging to the Lord' . . ." (Isaiah 44:5).

Ezekiel speaks in the same vein when he describes an Israel of the future. The Israel he knew was spiritually dead, a valley of bones. A day of spiritual resurrection was coming in which a new Israel would emerge—an Israel characterized by the presence of the Spirit:

> "Then you will know that I am the Lord,
> when I have opened your graves and caused
> you to come up out of your graves, My
> people.
> "And I will put My Spirit within you,
> and you will come to life, and I will place
> you on your own land. Then you will know
> that I, the Lord, have spoken and done it,"
> declares the Lord.
>
> Ezekiel 37:13-14

The new covenant that the Messiah was to accomplish would be brought to the heart of man by the Spirit.

228

It would be the Holy Spirit who would write the law within. "And I will put My Spirit within you and cause you to walk in My statutes, and you will be careful to observe My ordinances" (Ezekiel 36:27).

The abundance of peace that the kingdom of Messiah was always spoken of as having was also a result of the Spirit's work: "Until the Spirit is poured out upon us from on high, ... Then My people will live in a peaceful habitation, And in secure dwellings and in undisturbed resting places" (Isaiah 32:15,18).

Joel, one of the earliest prophets, had seen the day when the Spirit would be poured out upon all people, regardless of sex or station in life:

> And it will come about after this
> That I will pour out My Spirit on all mankind;
> And your sons and daughters will prophesy,
> Your old men will dream dreams,
> Your young men will see visions.
> And even on the male and female servants
> I will pour out My Spirit in those days.
>
> Joel 2:28-29

That time would be accompanied not only by supernatural gifts but by deliverance offered to those on Mount Zion:

> And it will come about that whoever calls on the name of the Lord
> Will be delivered.
>
> Joel 2:32

John the Baptist, the last prophet of the old order, had seen the crowning work of Messiah as immersing men into a vital relationship with the Spirit.

Thus all the prophets joined in declaring the age of Messiah as the activity of the Spirit among men. Jesus' last words to His disciples had been that the culmination of His work would be the giving of the Spirit.

It would be the Spirit who would bring into men's hearts the holy Law of God and shed abroad the love of the Lamb. The Spirit would unite with the hearts of men and so unite them with the king from whom He came. Thus one-with-the-Spirit people would live in the glory of God from whence the Lamb ruled. In the experience of the Spirit, Mount Zion would be on earth. With eyes opened and hearts flooded with light by the Spirit, people would know they belonged to the Lord in a union that was rooted in God's unchangeable holiness. They would respond in joyful worship and doxologies of praise. Without the Spirit's activity on earth the accomplishment of Jesus is the most fantastic theory ever told to humanity.

The resurrection and ascension of Jesus must never be seen as merely the bringing of a dead man to life. It was that, but more. It was the bringing to the world a new age. A new life was available to humanity in which all might become a son of God. As in Psalms 118:23-24:

> This is the Lord's doing;
> It is marvelous in our eyes.
> This is the day which the Lord has made;
> Let us rejoice and be glad in it.

The One who had justly put away sin, crushed the serpent, was now alive out of death, its Lord and conqueror. He was crowned with glory and honor, granted all authority to rule the universe through a new Israel that shared His life and power through the Spirit.

Even as heaven shouted the praises of the Lamb, Mary burst in on the distraught disciples and shouted that Jesus was alive—she had seen Him and touched Him. She was the first on earth to echo back the psalms of the heavens.

An embarrassed disciple coughed nervously, wishing this hallucinating woman would go away and get some sleep. Others smiled sadly. First there were hysterical reports of angels at the tomb, now a half-crazed woman who said she had seen the man they buried. It was time a man with common sense took control.

The disciples turned away to pick up the shattered remnants of their lives. They would try to begin again. But there was no goal left for them—no purpose to living.

24

Convinced Disciples

The disciples had decided to leave in the early afternoon to be home before darkness fell. There was nothing to stay for, but nothing to go home to either. Two of them dragged their feet aimlessly along the dusty road to Emmaus. It was only a few days since they had traveled eagerly into Jerusalem in the full expectancy that Jesus would declare Himself as Messiah. Their dreams of Israel's glory had evaporated in the stench of blood at Golgotha. They could talk of nothing but their shattered hopes.

The kindly voice of someone near interrupted and startled them because they hadn't heard any footsteps: "What are these words that you are exchanging with one another as you are walking?" (Luke 24:17).

They stopped and stared at the stranger. The question amazed them, especially Cleopas—his whole world had collapsed into one pile of fragments labeled "Jesus Messiah Dead." He supposed all Jerusalem was in mourning with him. He blurted out, "Are You the only one visiting Jerusalem and unaware of the things which have happened here in these days?" (Luke 24:18).

The stranger wrinkled His brow. "What things?" (Luke 24:19). The disciples were eager to talk about them. This was the first person they had been able to speak to who wasn't drowned in sorrow along with them.

> So they said to Him, "The things about Jesus the Nazarene, who was a prophet mighty in deed and word in the sight of God and all the people,
>
> "and how the chief priests and our rulers delivered Him up to the sentence of death, and crucified Him.
>
> "But we were hoping that it was He who was going to redeem Israel. Indeed, besides all this, it is the third day since these things happened.
>
> "But also some women among us amazed us. When they were at the tomb early in the morning,
>
> "and did not find His body, they came, saying that they had also seen a vision of angels, who said that He was alive.
>
> "And some of those who were with us went to the tomb and found it just exactly as the women also had said; but Him they did not see."
>
> Luke 24:19-24

They had continued to walk on towards Emmaus, and the crunch of their sandals on the sandy road was all that could be heard. Then the stranger spoke again—gently, yet with a tone of rebuke that they found themselves willing to receive: "O foolish men and slow of heart to believe in all that the prophets have spoken! Was it not necessary for the Christ to suffer these things and to enter into His glory?" (Luke 24:25-26).

Somewhere deep within the two disciples a flicker of life sputtered where death had settled in three days ago. The Messiah *supposed to suffer?* Enter into glory, yes; but suffer? They threw glances at one another, questions and hope showing on their faces. They could not register that the scenes they had witnessed and heard of this weekend had been the purpose of God.

The stranger began to enlarge on His statement from the books of Moses. The ancient promise to the human race of a triumphant deliverer with a bruised heel, and the promises to Abraham, Isaac, and Jacob. He asked their understanding of the blood of the sacrifices that flowed each day in the temple according to Levitical laws. Before man could enter through his representative into the glory of the holy of holies there had to be animal suffering and shedding of blood. He moved on to the prophets, quoting passages so familiar but bringing a light to them that made old words come alive, explaining that the Messiah was not only to have a glorious reign, but was also to be the suffering sacrificial Lamb to take away the sin of His subjects.

His words soothed their tired, sad minds and then fired them with a holy joy. Maybe the women were right. Maybe He was risen and had been at the tomb that morning . . . maybe. Sudden joy and a desire to live and tell the world what they were hearing burned inside them. They felt washed inside, alive; despair had gone.

A new world that had already dawned in the heavens now began to dawn within them. "But for you who fear My name the sun of righteousness will rise with healing in its wings; and you will go forth and skip about like calves from the stall" (Malachi 4:2).

235

They were at their gate all too soon. Long shadows were thrown across the street from the setting sun. The stranger was bidding them farewell, but the two disciples had to hear more. They constrained Him to eat with them and stay the night.

At the meal, the stranger took the bread and blessed it. Then He broke it and handed it to them. Suddenly they knew who this One was. *He was Jesus Messiah, the Lord of glory.* It was as if they had always known, yet now they were seeing Him for the first time. Then He was gone. The broken bread on the table was the only proof someone had been there a second before. They leaped to their feet and almost shouted to one another in voices that rippled with a joy from another world: "Were not our hearts burning within us while He was speaking to us on the road, while He was explaining the Scriptures to us?" (Luke 24:32).

It was not the end but the beginning. The long awaited kingdom was here and now.

The news could not be kept. Even though darkness had fallen they had to share what they had seen and heard. They ran along the road in uninhibited joy. Along this route David had leaped and danced a thousand years before as be brought the ark to Jerusalem and pitched his tabernacle on Zion. He had stood before the gates of Jerusalem and sung his psalm.

> Lift up your heads, O gates,
> And be lifted up, O ancient doors,
> That the King of glory may come in!
> Who is the King of glory?
> The Lord strong and mighty,
> The Lord mighty in battle.

Lift up your heads, O gates,
And lift them up, O ancient doors,
That the King of glory may come in!
Who is this King of glory?
The Lord of hosts,
He is the King of glory.

Psalms 24:7-10

The ark was a symbol of the Lord of glory. The Lord of glory had come in flesh, joined to humanity. He had worked in Nazareth, walked on the roads of Israel; they had eaten with Him, laughed with Him. Now He was risen from the dead and had entered into the heavens of which Jerusalem was a symbol to reign from the true Zion over the universe. *And that Lord of glory had sat in their house an hour ago.*

Their joy as they rushed through the gates of the city was David's joy filled to the full. They ran through the narrow streets of the dark city and burst in on the gathered disciples. They were oblivious of the grief that may have been there, nor did they apologize for such gaiety at the aftermath of a funeral . They shouted, "The Lord has really risen" (Luke 24:34).

Then He was there. He didn't walk through the door. He was just *there*. The babble of voices fell silent and the men backed away. It was one thing to hear of a living corpse from others, it was another to see Him standing in the room, appearing out of nowhere. The two who had met Him on the road to Emmaus that day could not bring themselves to familiarity; they realized that before them was the Man who was God.

He said, "Peace be with you" (John 20:26). They backed away, a strange terror gripping them.

He smiled at them. "Why are you troubled, and why do doubts arise in your hearts? See My hands and My

237

feet, that it is I Myself; touch Me and see, for a spirit does not have flesh and bones as you see that I have" (Luke 24:38-39).

He extended His hands. They saw the holes in His wrists where nails had been, and His feet bore a similar hole. This was the same Jesus who had suffered, now glorious. Their minds tried to grasp it, but all they could do was gasp for joy and wonder.

He interrupted their rapture. "Have you anything here to eat?" (Luke 24:41). Someone went and brought in the remains of the evening meal, broiled fish. They stared woodenly at Him as He ate it in front of them. Whatever form His body was, it was not a phantom spirit, but a tangible reality that could eat—a body like theirs, yet able to transcend all that they had known as fixed laws of the universe.

They relaxed. So it was true—He was alive. They sat around Him, as in the old days, and He began to teach them: "These are My words which I spoke to you while I was still with you, that all things which are written about Me in the Law of Moses and the Prophets and the Psalms must be fulfilled" (Luke 24:44).

It was as if their minds were opened to vistas of truth unseen until now. Though Caiaphas had machinated His death and Pilate had carried it out, it had been God's eternal purpose. He had died to bring about the blessing promised to Abraham, and the kingdom promised to the descendant of David.

Then He stood and came toward them: "Peace be with you; as the Father has sent Me, I also send you" (John 20:21). They were going into the world to *tell,* even as He had come to *do.* They would tell of what He had done. He bent over each one and breathed on him and said, "Receive the Holy Spirit" (John 20:22).

It was a definite act. His words were with awesome authority. He was actively willing that they should receive of the Spirit He had so recently been granted authority to bestow. The Spirit came into them communicating His life, uniting them with Messiah.

What happened in His resurrection now happened within them. They were raised up out from the condemnation of sin, and Satan's authority fell away beneath their feet. They entered into the glory of the Father's presence, becoming inhabitants of two worlds at once. They knew the Father's love and knew that they were His sons. One of them remembered what Jesus had said the night before He was arrested: "In that day you shall know that I am in My Father, and you in Me, and I in you. . . . If anyone loves Me, he will keep My word; and My Father will love him, and We will come to him, and make Our abode with him" (John 14:20, 23).

They had been born out of spiritual death—born again within. This company was the first of the dry bones to come alive knowing the word of God's Good News in the Messiah, and the life-bestowing breath of the Spirit. In that room in Jerusalem, Ezekiel's prophecy began to be fulfilled. A new Israel was coming into being whose mark was the Spirit of the Lord Messiah within them. The task of the old Israel was over.

The Lord went on to outline their work as they were joined to Him: "If you forgive the sins of any, their sins have been forgiven them; if you retain the sins of any, they have been retained" (John 20:23).

He had told them how man's sins were forgiven—it was through what He had done. That only way of forgiveness was now in their mouths to share with the world. He summed up the pivotal evening:

> "Thus it is written, that the Christ should suffer and rise again from the dead the third day;
>
> "and that repentance for forgiveness of sins should be proclaimed in His name to all the nations, beginning from Jerusalem.
>
> "You are witnesses of these things.
>
> "And behold, I am sending forth the promise of My Father upon you; but you are to stay in the city until you are clothed with power from on high."
>
> Luke 24:46-49

Then He was gone, even as He came.

A new fearless joy possessed them. They didn't bother to double-check the doors that night. *Who could kill people who had just been raised from the dead at the source of their true selves?* Who feared death when they had met the first one to rise out of death in a real and glorious body?

It was difficult to explain to Thomas. He had not been with them that night, preferring to weep alone. His mind worked only in cold, hard logic. Facts he must have. They sat around him, all seeking to talk at once and explain what had taken place. Thomas was threatened. Very obviously he had missed something that had affected all the others to the depth of their being. He shrugged. "Unless I shall see in His hands the imprint of the nails, and put my finger into the place of the nails, and put my hand into His side, I will not believe" (John 20:25).

It was seven days before they saw Him again. This time Thomas was with them. As before, Christ was just *there*—and before any could catch their breath He said, "Peace be with you" (John 20:26).

Thomas was shaken and white. It was to Him that Christ turned: "Reach here your finger, and see My hands, and reach here your hand, and put it into My side; and be not unbelieving, but believing" (John 20:27).

Someone gasped. The Lord hadn't been there when Thomas had expressed his doubts—*or had He?*

Did it mean that they did not have to see Him for Him to be present? Did it mean that He was always there, just sometimes visible?

He spoke further with them over the weeks of their union with Him. It was a union whereby, in their going into all the world with this Good News, it would be that He went into all the world. As they went, the kingdom would overspread the earth.

Their minds staggered. They were a group of common workers in the midst of a world that religiously and politically had crucified Him. Into that world they were to go and proclaim that the kingdom had come and that all were to repent and enter it. They went in His name, invested with His authority. And it was as if He went. Such was their union with Him, that for them to speak was to listen to Him. For them to see the sick and broken was for Him to see them—and as their hands touched them, it was the same Spirit that had acted through Him that would act through them.

The words from the upper room echoed: "Truly, truly, I say to you, he who believes in Me, the works that I do shall he do also; and greater works than these shall he do; because I go to the Father" (John 14:12).

Everything He had accomplished was now to be *worked out*. The kingdom of darkness was crushed; now they were to go as ambassadors of the newly crowned Lord of the universe and proclaim that fact. As they proclaimed it ,there would follow in their wake signs of supernatural character that proved He was alive and king.

He earnestly pressed upon them. They felt the urgency of His tone:

"Go into all the world and preach the gospel to all creation.

"He who has believed and has been baptized shall be saved; but he who has disbelieved shall be condemned.

"And these signs will accompany those who have believed: in My name they will cast out demons, they will speak with new tongues;

"they will pick up serpents, and if they drink any deadly poison, it shall not hurt them; they will lay hands on the sick, and they will recover."

Mark 16:15-18

25

The Kingdom Come

Forty days had passed since the women had come running with stories of an empty tomb. Throughout that time the Lord had appeared and taught them many thing about the kingdom of God on earth.

On this day, they were gathered in Bethany according to His direction the previous time He had been with them. The eleven apostles were there and the women who had been with Him throughout His earthly ministry. These had seen Him and been taught by Him for the last six weeks. Along with these were some others who wondered at what they saw and were confused at what they heard.

His message during the forty days had in-creasingly been about the Holy Spirit who would come. He was already *in them*, but within a few days they would be immersed *into Him*. Only then would the ecstatic disciples actually function as the covenant community on earth, the new Israel, inheritors of the blessing of Abraham.

Jesus reminded them that John had seen this as the goal: "For John baptized with water, but you shall be baptized with the Holy Spirit not many days from now" (Acts 1:5).

Some of the disciples who had not been in His teaching over the last weeks shifted awkwardly. They were confused. Was the resurrected Messiah now going to oust the Romans and lead Israel to glory? They asked, "Lord, is it at this time You are restoring the kingdom to Israel?" (Acts 1:6). Jesus took the questioners back to what He had just been speaking of, the baptism with the Holy Spirit. *The time when the glory of Israel that the prophets had spoken about would come was coincident with the coming of Spirit.* The timing of when the kingdom age would come into full effect in the world was in the hands of the Father—but they would know, for they would receive the power of the Spirit upon them.

He looked around at them. There was finality in His gaze, for this would be the last time they would see, with natural eyes, the king of the universe. He was going from the earth's dimension, and the Holy Spirit was coming to take His place. "All authority has been given to Me in heaven and on earth. Go therefore and make disciples of all the nations, baptizing them in the name of the Father and the Son and the Holy Spirit, teaching them to observe all that I commanded you; and lo, I am with you always, even to the end of the age" (Matthew 28:18-20).

The public entrance into the kingdom was to be by baptism. The expression, "the name" was familiar to Jews. It was a synonym for the unspeakable name of the

Lord God of Israel. Jesus was stating that henceforth the one God whom they worshiped as Jehovah was to be known in three persons: Father, Son, and Spirit.

The kingdom Jesus had brought into being was not something apart from the Israel that sprang from Abraham, but rather its fullness. The Israel of the patriarchs, kings, and prophets was the shadow—Jesus the Messiah and those joined to Him by the Spirit, were the *substance*. Israel after the flesh, of ethnic origin, was the root—and the Israel found in the Spirit was the flower that the root had always anticipated. Henceforth, God's chosen people, the children of His promises, were those joined to the promised One, His chosen Man, Jesus Christ.

So the announcement of one God in three persons was the unveiling of who the God of Israel truly was. They were to go and call the world to enter the Israel of the Spirit through faith in the saving action of the triune God.

The time had come for His departure before the eyes of the watching disciples. They would see the king in His glory. He lifted His hands in blessing. It was a familiar sight to them, for the high priest of Israel blessed the congregation of Israel in that fashion. In Israel the king and priest were two separate offices, but in Messiah the two offices were joined in final expression. He was the king who lifted His hands in high priestly blessing.

The Psalms had spoken that the day of His coronation would be His appointment as a high priest forever after the order of Melchizedek. The old order of Aaron was over, finding all it spoke of in the anointed Jesus.

Their priest-king blessed them, and as He did so was taken from them, slowly, majestically, into a cloud. Their gaze was riveted on Him—men who lived in the visible world ruled by the king from the invisible world. But a king who was truly man, who had eaten with them after His resurrection, whose tangible body was now going into the invisible heavens.

Wherever they were He was there, the king over them, the priest, to be their strength and the final revelation of truth, the light of the world. They were in a kingdom that was firmly grounded in this world, but not of it, having its origin, direction, and strength from the heavens.

Their mesmerized gaze was interrupted by a puzzled voice: "Men of Galilee, why do you stand looking into the sky? This Jesus, who has been taken up from you into heaven, will come in just the same way as you have watched Him go into heaven" (Acts 1:11).

The kingdom had come—and one day its king would return as He had gone, to consummate that kingdom and hand it over to the Father. Until then, He had told them exactly what they were to do.

They went slowly down the Mount of Olives to await whatever was meant by the baptism with the Holy Spirit and being endued with power from on high.

26

River of Life

Ezekiel had been the prophet that held hope out to Israel while they were in captivity, assuring them of a restoration that was surely coming to them. They would return to their land from the lands of their captivity, and they would rebuild the temple that had been torn down. After that, Ezekiel saw God granting them a shepherd king to reign over them after they had been infused with new life.

Each time a house of worship was constructed, God gave the plans in great detail—for each pin, board, and curtain spoke of God's saving purpose. So Moses was given every dimension of the tabernacle, which takes up half the Book of Exodus. When the tabernacle was replaced by Solomon's temple, David was given the exact plan that Solomon had to follow. It is no surprise then to find that when Solomon's temple was destroyed, Ezekiel was given in great detail the plans for the next temple, which was to be built by the returning exiles. He described the plans in chapters 40 to 47 of his book. In his vision, having described this temple, he saw a strange phenomenon. From out of the temple flowed a supernatural river of life, bringing life wherever it flowed.

The exiles *did* return, they *did* build a temple. It was embellished by Herod and was the one that Jesus taught in. But the final part of the prophecy of Ezekiel awaited fulfillment, for no supernatural river had ever flowed out of it. During one feast in that temple Jesus referred to Ezekiel's prophecy: "If any man is thirsty, let him come to Me and drink. He who believes in Me, as the Scripture said, 'From his innermost being shall flow rivers of living water'" (John 7:37-38).

Ezekiel was the only prophet that spoke of rivers of living water. The rivers of living water was a reference to the Holy Spirit to be given after Jesus was glorified.

The disciples had seen Him suffer and be glorified; now they awaited the coming of the Spirit. The reading of the psalms and prophets by the priests took on new meaning now, for they had been shown their true meaning by the One who was the only subject of those Scriptures. With great joy they blessed and praised God for fulfilling all His promises. During this time they lived in Jerusalem, praying together in the large upper room of the house. They were waiting for they knew not what in obedience to their Lord Messiah. But could anything be greater than what they had discovered in Him?

The city of Jerusalem was all preparation again, this time for the feast of Pentecost, otherwise called the Feast of Weeks. It fell fifty days after Passover, hence, *Pentecost* (Greek *pentekoste*, fiftieth day). It was the thanksgiving for harvest, when two loaves made from the grain of the new harvest were offered to the Lord in thanksgiving.

The day of the feast fell ten days after Jesus had passed from their sight into the heavens. That morning the disciples, some one hundred and twenty of them, were at the temple for the first services of the day. During the intermission before other services began, they were sitting together praising God for what they knew through their risen Messiah. They did not know that the last Pentecost was about to happen, the Pentecost that all the others had foreshadowed and waited for. All that this feast signified was about to find its historic fulfillment.

As they were sitting together between services, a little before nine o'clock in the morning, a sound of wind was heard, so loud that it could be heard through the entire city. It was centered in the particular house in which they were sitting, probably Solomon's Porch. The atmosphere became a glowing, radiant, flashing tongue of what appeared to be fire. It quickly separated and sat upon each disciple, engulfing him in its glory. The wonder of God's love, His holy salvation in Jesus, was made known to them in such a fashion that they all began praising God out of a depth they never had before.

Within the speech centers of their brain came languages they had never learned, sounds they had never been taught to pronounce. They began speaking them, and as they did more were given. They found the new language caught up their whole

249

being in an adoration of God they had never experienced before. It was as if every yearning and cry of the spirit to adequately praise God was answered. They were free as birds to climb on and on into the heavens in praise, adoring, and psalming the God of their salvation even though their minds could not comprehend what was being said. All that the singing of choirs in the temple had sought to say and all that David's worship in Zion had wrestled to express, now cascaded out of the spirits of these men who were engulfed in the glory of God's Holy Spirit. They were in an ecstasy that was transdimensional. In body and soul they were on earth, but in spirit they were in the holy of holies.

In the temple of Ezekiel's vision the rivers of living water were bubbling up, coming out through the men who were the subjects of the king. Soon, from the temple the living water would flow to the ends of the earth, healing all it touched.

The noise of what had sounded like a violent wind had caused everyone in Jerusalem to fear. Pilgrims from every nation, as well as the populace, did what every pious Jew would do on such an occasion. They ran to the temple.

A crowd had gathered around the praising disciples. Bewilderment showed on the faces of the onlookers, who were mostly pilgrims. They were hearing men and women who were obviously ignorant Galileans speaking fluently in the dialects they spoke at home. They turned to each other, puzzled: "Why, are not all these who are speaking Galileans? And how is it that we each hear them in our own language to which we were born? . . .

we hear them in our own tongues speaking of the mighty deeds of God" (Acts 2:7-8, 11).

A fear and excitement mingled in them. Those in the crowd were jostling one another to see these people who looked too overwhelmed with joy to be merely enjoying a part of the ritual. "What does this mean?" they asked each other (Acts 2:12). Some just laughed and turned their backs, trying to get out of the crowd that was growing every moment. They mocked the one hundred and twenty hilarious people: "They are full of sweet wine" (Acts 2:13).

In his ecstasy, Peter heard the mocking and knew it was time for an explanation. He addressed the crowd in the common language that all understood. What they were beholding was the fulfillment of Joel's prophecy. The Spirit had been poured out upon all flesh, for the man so recently crucified had been made Lord of all. The rule of Jesus from the heavens was understood on earth in the outpoured Spirit. Said Peter:

> "Men of Israel, listen to these words: Jesus the Nazarene, a man attested to you by God with miracles and wonders and signs which God performed through Him in your midst, just as you yourselves know—
>
> "this Man, delivered up by the predetermined plan and foreknowledge of God, you nailed to a cross by the hands of godless men and put Him to death.
>
> "And God raised Him up again, putting an end to the agony of death, since it was impossible for Him to be held in its power. . . .

> "This Jesus God raised up again, to
> which we are all witnesses.
>
> "Therefore having been exalted to the
> right hand of God, and having received from
> the Father the promise of the Holy Spirit, He
> has poured forth this which you both see and
> hear. . . .
>
> "Therefore let all the house of Israel
> know for certain that God has made Him
> both Lord and Christ—this Jesus whom you
> crucified."
>
> Acts 2:22-24, 32-33, 36

It was done, all that the prophets had spoken. Men born of the Spirit through the accomplishment of the Messiah had now entered into the Holy Spirit. He was the dimension in which they lived and moved. As the baptism of John had placed people into the medium of water, so the baptism of the Messiah placed the believers into the sphere of the Holy Spirit. John had administered his baptism; and Jesus, said Peter, from the glory of the heavens had ministered this one.

In the state of being filled with the Spirit, they were aware of their union with the Triune God through the Lord Jesus. They were aware of living in the glorious presence while still on earth and were given a language to express their spirits to God.

In that condition, the Spirit worked through them on earth, even as He had done without measure through Jesus. They knew things known only to the Spirit, if He chose to tell them. They could decide with a wisdom beyond all the calculations of earth. Faced with Satanic opposition, they could not be deceived; from the sphere of the Spirit they were enabled to clearly discern whence the deception came. The sick were given gifts of healing at the speaking of their words, and miracles took place. They were the expressers of the Spirit's power who were now actively bringing men into the kingdom of the Messiah.

The Spirit was supplying Peter with a clarity of thought and expression, bringing to his remembrance the words Jesus had taught him. Through this man, the Spirit was calling to the multitude to enter the kingdom. It was not only a proclaiming of the truth, the Good News in logical fashion, but it was an activity of the Spirit in those spoken words. These men were the body through which the Spirit expressed Himself.

The result was a terror that seized the gathered crowd. Their cry rose to the point where Peter could hear them. It was as if their world had been cut in two by a great sword, and they cried out, "Brethren, what shall we do?" (Acts 2:37).

What the one hundred twenty had received was for everyone throughout the ages until Messiah Jesus returned again. Peter commanded them:

> "Repent, and let each of you be baptized in the name of Jesus Christ for the forgiveness of your sins; and you shall receive the gift of the Holy Spirit.
> "For the promise is for you and your children, and for all who are far off, as many as the Lord our God shall call to Himself."
> Acts 2:38-39

Repent. The word means to change the mind. The crowd had looked upon Jesus as a blasphemer, a peasant claiming to be the Son of God. This was the basis for their crucifying Him. The Resurrection had proved Him to be all He had claimed. It meant that His death was very different from what they had supposed. He had died bearing the sin of others and raised because their penalty was exhausted. Change your mind concerning this man called Jesus. He has been made Lord and Christ. The call was to exit the kingdom of self-grasping self, the authority of the lie and darkness, and to come under the rule of the One who was now glorified.

This decision they were to express in *baptism.* Baptism was the method by which faith acted. It said, "He took my place and died for me, as me. He carried my sins and my sinful way of life into the wrath of God, for that is where they belong. God was right and just in so doing. I accept that and receive it. Now I am burying that old self-loving way of life and publicly declaring that Jesus Messiah rules my life from the throne of God." Upon that, said Peter, you too will receive the *gift of the Spirit* even as we.

This was "the promise." The promise could only refer to just one promise, which every Jew awaited. It was the blessing of Abraham promised two millenniums before and now in the temple on the day of Pentecost finally brought in fullness into man's history. Sinner man could be justified and granted the Spirit through the seed of Abraham. The people responded to Peter's command with joy and about three thousand souls entered the kingdom that day. The bones of death valley were coming together and a great army of resurrected ones was beginning to take form.

27

Persecutor Become Disciple

The river of life that was contained in the riverbed of the one hundred twenty had become larger and deeper , having three thousand more flow through. It flowed out into the streets of Jerusalem, proclaiming the resurrection of Jesus and therefore the nature of His death.

Not only did these people claim a mystical relationship with Jesus Messiah, but the sick were healed and demons were cast out—miracles took place in His name. *It was like having Jesus back in Jerusalem, only multiplied now a hundred times.* At times, Caiaphas' mouth became dry at what he heard, feeling that he was meeting the man he had put to death.

If only he could have produced the body and proved He was a corpse, the whole thing would be over in a few days. Instead, these men who a few months ago had been conspicuous by their absence at the crucifixion were proclaiming His resurrection a few hundred feet from the empty tomb. After a lame man had been healed, bringing thousands more under the Lordship of Jesus, the chief priests arrested the preachers and threw them into jail overnight. The next day they stood on trial before the council.

It was Peter, speaking under the inspiration of the Spirit, who answered the judges:

> "Rulers and elders of the people,
> "if we are on trial today for a benefit done to a sick man, as to how this man has been made well,
> "let it be known to all of you, and to all the people of Israel, that by the name of Jesus Christ the Nazarene, whom you crucified, whom God raised from the dead—by this name this man stands here before you in good health.
> "He is the STONE WHICH WAS REJECTED by you, THE BUILDERS, but WHICH BECAME THE VERY CORNER stone.
> "And there is salvation in no one else— for there is no other name under heaven that has been given among men, by which we must be saved."
>
> Acts 4:8-12

There was nothing to do, and no reason to punish them—and so, reluctantly, they let them go.

During the months that lengthened into a couple of years, the growing company who claimed Jesus as Messiah met in the temple and saw themselves as part of Judaism. The old Israel held in its womb the new Israel of the Spirit.

Two men saw that the followers of Jesus Messiah could never coexist with the old Israel. Both of the men attended the synagogue in Jerusalem attended by Cilician Jews. Stephen was a believer in Jesus as Lord and Messiah. Saul was a Pharisee among Pharisees. To him, the way of approach to God was an arduous affair ,but simple in its basics. Each morning he thanked God he was a Jew and not a Gentile. Then, as a Jew, he took the Law and did all in his power to keep it, weaving it into every area of his life. He was particularly proud of his accomplishments in this—he did it so well that he was without blame. As to forgiveness, that was handled by the constant blood sacrifices in the temple—although he never felt in great need of that.

When Saul heard Stephen's message concerning Jesus, his brilliant mind came directly to the point. If Jesus was the Messiah, then ultimately all he believed in was finished. This was no sect within Judaism, as the Pharisees were, but something that brought the whole system to an end.

As a Pharisee, he was repulsed by the message. How could the Messiah of glory be nailed to a cross and so be the cursed of God? As to the Resurrection, he chose to believe the stories of the soldiers. The interpretation Stephen put on the whole thing—that this Jesus was the final sacrifice for all men—disgusted him.

It disgusted him so much that he moved from debate to treachery. One day Stephen found himself arrested and hauled away to stand trial before the Great Sanhedrin for blasphemy. The eyes of seventy-one members of the Great Sanhedrin were on him: "Are these things so?" (Acts 7:1).

The face of Stephen was almost radiant, he seemed to be reflecting another world. He began to deliver his defense, following the purpose of God through the history of the nation of Israel. The judges became visibly angry—some were white-faced with rage. Stephen stopped his oration of the history of the nation and addressed the men in front of him:

> "You men who are stiff-necked and uncircumcised in heart and ears are always resisting the Holy Spirit; you are doing just as your fathers did.
>
> "Which one of the prophets did your fathers not persecute? And they killed those who had previously announced the coming of the Righteous One, whose betrayers and murderers you have now become;
>
> "you who received the law as ordained by angels, and yet did not keep it."
>
> Acts 7:51-53

They rose from their seats in open fury. Stephen appeared not to see them, aware only that he was in the Spirit. The visible universe rolled back and the invisible became visible to him. He cried out, "Behold, I see the heavens opened up and the Son of Man standing at the right hand of God" (Acts 7:56).

It was enough! In a frenzy, they rushed from their seats and dragged him from the temple, through the streets, pulling his body over the stones to the Rock of Execution outside the city where they stoned blasphemers. Picking up stones, they began to hurl them at him, tearing and breaking his body. Saul, the instigator, pulled his blue robe close and stood by the clothes of the executioners.

Saul curled his lip at the young man dying in front of him—all for the sake of a dead blasphemer who called Himself the Messiah. Fool! In that moment he dedicated himself to wiping the name of Jesus of Nazareth from the minds of men and saving Judaism from shame.

As Saul raged within, Stephen looked up toward heaven and prayed, "Lord Jesus, receive my spirit!" (Acts 7:59). He fell into a kneeling position and prayed for his executioners, "Lord, do not hold this sin against them!" (Acts 7:60).

Saul sucked in his breath. The blasphemer was praying for him. He was praying to the despised Nazarene. Saul knew why he was doing that. Stephen had made it plain that he saw man's sins laid upon Jesus, who bore them away forever. Stephen was agreeing with the Nazarene in his prayer, that he too saw the sins of Saul and the others dealt with through that one sacrifice on the cross.

Blind with rage, disgusted and repulsed, Saul turned away to implement his dedication to wiping that accursed name from the earth. He met with the two chief priests, Annas and Caiaphas, who saw in this raging young man the savior of the temple. They gave him the authority to purge Jerusalem of all who confessed Jesus as Lord and Messiah.

The new subjects of the Lord Jesus were hauled into the synagogue to answer to Saul. There it was demanded that they curse the name of Jesus, instead, they began to speak of Him. Their words came with the wisdom Saul had heard in Stephen.

They were flogged within seconds of death, thrown into dungeons, and some were stoned. Again and again Saul heard the stories Jesus told, the miracles He performed, and the claims He made. He looked into the eyes of men and women who calmly claimed to have met Him after His resurrection. All of them prayed for him and most of them went on their way rejoicing after being beaten.

It never occurred to them to question the absolute reign of Christ, even though they were being beaten. Saul thought it a joke that they claimed to be the fulfillment of the glorious promises made to Israel, yet were beaten and jailed. They knew the glory of God at the center of their existence. They also knew that the prophets had spoken of a kingdom that would exist in the midst of the king's enemies.

News began to trickle in. The heretics had fled Jerusalem and had gone north to Samaria and Damascus carrying their doctrine with them. Still raging, Saul went to the high priest for authority to carry his inquisition to Damascus.

It was a spring day as the band of men moved along the road to Damascus. Suddenly, Saul and his company found themselves on the ground, paralyzed. It was not a flash, like lightning, but a steady light from an awesome source beyond the visible world. Then a voice that spoke in Saul's language came out of the light: "Saul, Saul, why are you persecuting Me?" (Acts 26:14).

Looking up, Saul saw a man in the center of the awful light—a man about his own age. It flashed across his mind that this was Jesus—but that could never be, for that blasphemer was dead. He replied, "Who art Thou, Lord?" The young man answered him, "I am Jesus whom you are persecuting" (Acts 26:15).

All his persecution against these simple folk was put into perspective. He had been seeking to kill Jesus the whole time. Jesus was claiming that He was in such a unity with His subjects that for them to be persecuted was to persecute Him. Saul's intellect could not put it together but he knew that he had met Jesus, and without explanation, that changed everything. Henceforth he was the slave of this person.

The young King of the Universe continued speaking:

> "But arise, and stand on your feet; for this purpose I have appeared to you, to appoint you a minister and a witness not only to the things which you have seen, but also to the things in which I will appear to you;
>
> "delivering you from the Jewish people and from the Gentiles, to whom I am sending you,
>
> "to open their eyes so that they may turn from darkness to light and from the dominion of Satan to God, in order that they may

> receive forgiveness of sins and an inheritance
> among those who have been sanctified by
> faith in Me."
>
> Acts 26:16-18

Saul obeyed—and as he stumbled to his feet, realized he was blind. A light shone in his spirit while darkness held his physical eyes. They led him to the city. A house had already been rented by the local rabbis to accommodate the august visitor with letters from the high priest. It was a house on Straight Street owned by Judas.

The city was awaiting his arrival. The syna-gogues prepared for inquisitions; the confessors of Christ waited for the hatred of the present world. They all waited for a man who never came.

Saul of Tarsus was led to his room, and refused all food. Alone in physical darkness and spiritual light, he wrestled with the great questions that now confronted his intellect. His first problem brought tears to his blind eyes. The One he had raged against *loved him.* He would never get over that. Even on the Damascus road, He had not rebuked him, just arrested him into life.

Jesus was alive! He could not reconcile that with his intellect, *but he had met Him—alive, exalted in the heavens.* If He was alive, then His death took on new meaning. Hanging on the cross, certainly, He was the cursed of God, but not for sin of His own—it was for the sin of the world, and even for the sin of Saul of Tarsus. If He was risen, then Saul's sin was gone. He, the hater of Jesus, could be welcomed into the glorious presence as if he had never sinned, because of what Jesus had accomplished.

Across the city, a man continued to wait for the persecution that did not come. On this, the third day after Saul of Tarsus arrived, Ananias heard his Lord speak to him: "Ananias." He responded at once, "Behold, here am I, Lord" (Acts 9:10).

The voice instructed, "Arise, and go to the street called Straight, and inquire at the house of Judas for a man from Tarsus named Saul, for behold, he is praying, and he has seen in a vision a man named Ananias come in and lay his hands on him, so that he might regain his sight" (Acts 9:11-12).

Ananias hesitated, then answered, "Lord, I have heard from many about this man, how much harm he did to Thy saints at Jerusalem; and here he has authority from the chief priests to bind all who call upon Thy name" (Acts 9:13-14).

There was no explanation, just an affirmation of the command: "Go, for he is a chosen instrument of Mine, to bear My name before the Gentiles and kings and the sons of Israel; for I will show him how much he must suffer for My name's sake" (Acts 9:15-16).

Saul of Tarsus! One of us! A brother! One who was chosen of God to be His special ambassador-at-large. Surely this must be what Isaiah was speaking of:

> And the wolf will dwell with the lamb,
> And the leopard will lie down with the kid,
> And the calf and the young lion and the fatting together;
> And a little boy will lead them.
>
> Isaiah 11:6

In the house of Judas, Ananias stood nervously before the blind man who had come to this city to destroy him. Fearfully, he stretched out his hands and placed them on his head: "Brother Saul, the Lord Jesus, who appeared to you on the road by which you were coming, has sent me so that you may regain your sight, and be filled with the Holy Spirit" (Acts 9:17).

It was like scales fell from Saul's eyes. Not only healed in the physical, he was filled with the Spirit. Like all those before him he entered into that dimension of the Spirit under the Lordship of Jesus Messiah. Ananias took him and plunged him into the river in baptism, stating that his sins were gone through the accomplishment of the Christ.

28

The Supranational Nation

The early company of believers saw themselves as the fulfillment of the words of the prophets. They were the kingdom of Messiah on earth. But tradition dies hard. They still believed that the long-awaited kingdom was to be made up exclusively of members of the Jewish faith and nation. If a Gentile was to enter the kingdom, he would first have to become a convert to the Hebrew faith and culture.

The question had not been articulated but was taking shape among thinking disciples: Who is a candidate for the kingdom? Was it only devout Jews, or uncircumcised Gentiles, too?

It was a vague issue until Peter shocked the believers by going to proclaim the Good News to Cornelius, a Roman centurion in Caesarea. The very idea had been obnoxious to him, but at the command of the Holy Spirit, he had gone. Before Peter had finished speaking the Good News of God's kingdom among men, Cornelius and his household had believed and were filled with the Spirit and spoke in tongues as the original disciples had. Peter promptly baptized them in water, the outward seal that they were members of the kingdom of Messiah.

The leadership in Jerusalem was shocked at Peter and only grudgingly admitted that the Holy Spirit had commanded him.

Soon a group of disciples went to Antioch and proclaimed Jesus to everyone who cared to listen. Gentiles joined Jews and they entered together into the kingdom in the Holy Spirit.

Saul, who had returned to Tarsus, was called to help with the expanding group of believers in Antioch. He joined the group of elders and ministered in the city. What he had seen on the Damascus road had convinced him that the nature of the kingdom was supranational. The believers under the Lordship of Jesus were a new company the world had never seen, transcending nationality and finding their unity in the Lordship of Jesus.

The pagans of Antioch took note of these people who seemed to be a sect within Judaism. They listened and concluded that the message of these people centered around two things. One, someone called Christ was the center of life; and two, these people were His willing slaves. They nicknamed them *Christianos* (English, *Christians*), meaning "the slaves of Christ."

The animosity of the Jews increased. If the Hebrew Scriptures were fulfilled in a risen Messiah who now ruled the universe from the invisible throne, then there was no glorious kingdom on earth for the Jewish people. It meant that the chosen race had focused on a chosen man called Jesus, and the only glory for the Jew was to confess Him as Lord.

Opposition was also growing from another quarter—group who recognized Jesus as Messiah, but insisted that Gentiles must first be converted to Judaism before they could enter the kingdom of Messiah.

Saul, now called Paul, was sent, along with Barnabas, on a mission to Asia, to the region of Galatia, where they proclaimed Jesus as Lord in every town. In each place, many Jews and Gentiles accepted the Good News. The local Jews rose up against the message and bitterly persecuted Paul and the company he left behind.

Some time after he returned to Antioch, a company of preachers came from the area around Jerusalem, calling all of the believers in Antioch to be converted to Judaism. This was the final straw. Paul knew there had to be a confrontation in Jerusalem with the recognized Christian leaders.

Paul gathered with the elders at Jerusalem in counsel and each contributed to the issue. It was James who put it all into the context of the Scriptures. Under the illumination of the Spirit, he saw that the coming together of Jews and Gentiles under the reign of Christ was the fulfillment of the words of the prophet Amos.

> Brethren, listen to me.
> Simeon has related how God first concerned Himself about taking from among the Gentiles a people for His name.
> And with this the words of the prophets agree, just as it is written,

> " 'AFTER THESE THINGS I WILL RETURN, AND
> I WILL REBUILD THE TABERNACLE OF DAVID
> WHICH HAS FALLEN, AND I WILL REBUILD ITS
> RUINS, AND I WILL RESTORE IT,
>
> 'IN ORDER THAT THE REST OF MANKIND MAY
> SEEK THE LORD, AND ALL THE GENTILES WHO
> ARE CALLED BY MY NAME,'
>
> "Says the Lord, who makes these things
> known from of old."
>
> Acts 15:13-18

The tabernacle of David was being rebuilt. But the new Zion, the temple of the age of Messiah, was not to be made of bricks but of all nationalities vitally united to the Messiah.

Later Peter wrote of this:

> And coming to Him as to a living stone,
> rejected by men, but choice and precious in
> the sight of God,
>
> you also, as living stones, are being built
> up as a spiritual house for a holy priesthood,
> to offer up spiritual sacrifices acceptable to
> God through Jesus Christ.
>
> For this is contained in Scripture:
> "BEHOLD, I LAY IN ZION A CHOICE STONE, A
> PRECIOUS CORNER STONE, AND HE WHO BELIEVES
> IN HIM SHALL NOT BE DISAPPOINTED."
>
> 1 Peter 2:4-6

The men and women streaming into the kingdom of God from all nations were the ultimate reality of which the choirs of David, singing in rapture, were but the pointer. The council at Jerusalem parted with joy to tell the Gentiles that they were accepted into the kingdom without being converted to Judaism.

Others, however, left Jerusalem to step up their efforts to make new Gentile converts submit to circumcision and the Levitical Law. Word came to Paul that these pseudo-believers had spread their message throughout Galatia and caused great confusion among the new communities of believers.

Paul's incisive mind saw that this was but a symptom of a far greater heresy. He saw that the Good News itself was at stake. The issue went beyond the Jewish-Gentile struggle. The real question was, *How does a person become right with God?*

Was it through the accomplishment of Christ *alone,* or what He had done *plus* the struggles of a person to keep the Law? Was the redemptive work of Christ to be completed by the believer? No one, however, could satisfy the demands of God's law; but in Jesus' one act of sacrifice, sin had been taken. The believers in Jesus could now be accepted as if they had never sinned, the righteousness of God being given to them.

What Christ had done could only be received as a gift. This was the essence of faith for Paul—believers resting on what Christ had done in the midst of history.

He wrote to the struggling Galatians, his words pouring out like molten fire, ". . . nevertheless knowing that a man is not justified by the works of the Law but through faith in Christ Jesus, even we have believed in Christ Jesus, that we may be justified by faith in Christ, and not by the works of the Law; since by the works of the Law shall no flesh be justified" (Galatians 2:16).

But that raised the question: *Who was the seed of Abraham?* Was not the Jew the inheritor of all the blessings, making the Gentile, at best, a second-class citizen? Paul had once believed that, when he was a Pharisee. At that time in his thinking, there was no doubt as to the identity of the seed of Abraham. It was that nation of Israel that had the blood of Abraham, Isaac, and Jacob in its veins. Now all had changed in the light of Jesus Messiah. *The identification of the seed of Abraham was not a matter of blood in the veins, but faith in the heart.*

He wrote, "Even so Abraham BELIEVED GOD, AND IT WAS RECKONED TO HIM AS RIGHTEOUSNESS. Therefore, be sure that it is those who are of faith that are sons of Abraham" (Galatians 3:6-7).

Paul saw that the original promise to Abraham included all nations, and the inclusion of the Gentiles into the kingdom was the original plan. "And the Scripture, foreseeing that God would justify the Gentiles by faith, preached the gospel beforehand to Abraham, saying, ALL THE NATIONS SHALL BE BLESSED IN YOU. So then those who are of faith are blessed with Abraham, the believer" (Galatians 3:8-9).

One person had become the focal point of what God had done. Jesus had become the curse and made the promised blessing available to the whole earth.

> Christ redeemed us from the curse of the
> Law, having become a curse for us—for it
> is written, "CURSED IS EVERY ONE WHO HANGS
> ON A TREE"—
>
> in order that in Christ Jesus the blessing
> of Abraham might come to the Gentiles, so
> that we might receive the promise of the
> Spirit through faith.
>
> Galatians 3:13-14

The seed of Abraham was Jesus the Messiah, who
had become a curse for men: "Now the promises were
spoken to Abraham and to his seed. He does not say,
'AND TO SEEDS,' as referring to many, but rather to one,
'AND TO YOUR SEED,' that is, Christ" (Galatians 3:16).

But although the seed had narrowed to one person,
it broadened to include all who would submit themselves
to what had been accomplished in that One. Believers
were *united* to Christ, made one with the true seed. In
such a union the believers were the seed of Abraham
and inheritors of the promise.

> For you are all sons of God through faith
> in Christ Jesus.
>
> For all of you who were baptized into
> Christ have clothed yourselves with Christ.
>
> There is neither Jew nor Greek, there is
> neither slave nor free man, there is neither
> male nor female; for you are all one in Christ
> Jesus.
>
> And if you belong to Christ, then you are
> Abraham's offspring, heirs according to
> promise.
>
> Galatians 3:26-29

To Paul, this company was not an elite within Judaism, a spiritual counterpart to a natural Israel. The company of believers in Jesus Messiah were the *only* Israel—the finale of all God had promised since Abraham. They were a company where nationality, sex, status, and riches gave way to the common status of union with Messiah.

Paul preached this around the world and was followed by Jews seeking to convert Gentiles to Judaism. At the temple where Paul was visiting, a Jew from Ephesus, who recognized him, started a riot, accusing Paul of bringing a Gentile into the sacred precincts. So violent was the mob scene that soldiers poured out of the Tower of Antonia and arrested Paul.

Paul denied the charge, but pointed to the real reason:

> "But this I admit to you, that according to the Way which they call a sect I do serve the God of our fathers, believing everything that is in accordance with the Law, and that is written in the Prophets;
>
> "having a hope in God, which these men cherish themselves, that there shall certainly be a resurrection of both the righteous and the wicked."
>
> Acts 24:14-15

The Jews were seeking to destroy Paul on the charge he was overturning Judaism. His reply to them was that this new Way was the only Judaism the prophets saw. This was the hope that they cherished—it was the flower of the root that had been growing since God's first word to Adam.

The governor held Paul in a dungeon in Caesarea, and on a certain occasion had him speak before King Agrippa. In the course of his defense, Paul took up the same theme:

> "I am standing trial for the hope of the promise made by God to our fathers;
>
> "the promise to which our twelve tribes hope to attain, as they earnestly serve God night and day. And for this hope, O King, I am being accused by Jews.
>
> "Why is it considered incredible among you people if God does raise the dead?. . .
>
> "And so, having obtained help from God, I stand to this day testifying both to small and great, stating nothing but what the Prophets and Moses said was going to take place;
>
> "that the Christ was to suffer, and that by reason of His resurrection from the dead He should be the first to proclaim light both to the Jewish people and to the Gentiles."
>
> Acts 26:6-8, 22-23

From the dungeon in Caesarea, Paul was taken to Rome to stand trial before the emperor Nero. While awaiting trial in Rome, he was kept under house arrest and had plenty of time to meditate, pray, and write. He saw his sufferings as the means under God for bringing into emergence the new Israel that was composed of Jew and Gentile. So Paul wrote what many consider to be his most sublime doctrinal letter to a company of Gentile and Jewish believers in Ephesus:

Therefore remember, that formerly you, the Gentiles in the flesh, who are called "Uncircumcision" by the so-called "Circumcision, which is performed in the flesh by human hands—

remember that you were at that time separate from Christ, excluded from the commonwealth of Israel, and strangers to the covenants of promise, having no hope and without God in the world.

But now in Christ Jesus you who formerly were far off have been brought near by the blood of Christ.

For He Himself is our peace, who made both groups into one, and broke down the barrier of the dividing wall,

by abolishing in His flesh the enmity, which is the Law of commandments contained in ordinances, that in Himself He might make the two into one new man, thus establishing peace,

and might reconcile them both in one body to God through the cross, by it having put to death the enmity.

Ephesians 2:11-16

Both Jew and Gentile had to come the same way, Paul wrote. And having come into the dimension of the Spirit, they became the new temple Jesus had built in three days:

AND HE CAME AND PREACHED PEACE TO YOU WHO WERE FAR AWAY, AND PEACE TO THOSE WHO WERE NEAR;

for through him we both have our access in one Spirit to the Father.

276

> So then you are no longer strangers and
> aliens, but you are fellow-citizens with the
> saints, and are of God's household,
> having been built upon the foundation of
> the apostles and prophets, Christ Jesus
> Himself being the corner stone,
> in whom the whole building, being fitted
> together is growing into a holy temple in the
> Lord;
> in whom you also are being built toget-
> her into a dwelling of God in the Spirit.
>
> Ephesians 2:17-22

It was Paul's insistence that Messiah Jesus was
the glory of Israel, and that Jews and Gentiles
made up the kingdom spoken of by the prophets,
that had brought him to this jail.

> For this reason I, Paul, the prisoner of
> Christ Jesus for the sake of you Gentiles—
> . . . which [mystery of Christ] in other
> generations was not made known to the sons
> of men, as it has now been revealed in His
> holy apostles and prophets in the Spirit;
> to be specific, that the Gentiles are
> fellow-heirs and fellow-members of the
> body, and fellow-partakers of the promise in
> Christ Jesus through the gospel.
>
> Ephesians 3:1, 5-6

Here was the kingdom within all kingdoms. It
was a spiritual nation that was comprised of new
creatures in Christ Jesus who were called out from
all nations. It was the Church.

29

Life-Style of the Saved

The words of the psalmist reached their fullest expression in the Church of the new-born:

> When the Lord brought back the captive ones of Zion,
> We were like those who dream.
> Then our mouth was filled with laughter,
> And our tongue with joyful shouting;
> Then they said among the nations,
> "The Lord has done great things for them."
> The Lord has done great things for us;
> We are glad.
>
> Psalms 126:1-3

It *was* like a dream. The kingdom on earth, among men, in the Holy Spirit, under the rule of Messiah on His throne in heaven. At the very idea, their mouths were filled with laughter and gladness.

Coming under the rule of the Lord Jesus was only the beginning. When the laughter and gladness had been enjoyed, it had to be translated into life. They had truly entered the kingdom and were truly raised to life in the Spirit, but as yet it was only a dream as far as the effect on their actual life-style. What had happened by the grace of God had to be worked out in experience.

They had received within them the Spirit of Christ. It was that life they had beheld in the life of Jesus on earth. As a body, the Church, the true seed of Abraham, they were to be expressers of *that* life. The kingdom was the expression among men of the king Himself. They had come out of the darkness of self-will and independence from God, and stood blinking in the light of dependence upon Christ through the Spirit. What had been the great choice—to repent and rest in the work of another—was now to be worked out in their every choice.

All their understanding of life had been wrong. Every interpretation put upon life had been distorted. In coming to Christ, the center of life was changed. A rebirth took place. It was no longer the "I" of self-assertion, but Jesus Christ reigning within by the Spirit He placed there. In the light of that, every thought, attitude, and proceeding action has to be brought into line with the new center. The process begins out of the crisis of new birth. The rule begun in the center of the man must be established in the extremities of his life-style. His speech and even his memories must be brought under the authority of the light he has now seen in Christ.

Although he has entered the kingdom, his life is still disintegrated. From the moment of his new birth begins the process of *being* saved. The word *saved* means to put back together again, to be made whole in every part of the person.

It's a matter of being the person Christ has brought into being in the new birth. The believer must become in his life-style what he has already become in his union with Messiah. Paul called upon the Philippians to, "work out your salvation with fear and trembling; for it is God who is at work in you, both to will and to work for His good pleasure" (Philippians 2:12-13). It was because God was working in them that they were to work out the integration. He was working internally what they must then work externally.

In the light of the ascended Jesus, all that man thought to be normal, is seen to be death. The accepted way of life was found to be insanity in the light of truth. With the entrance of the Spirit of Christ, man is born again and God's love is shed abroad in his heart. United with God, who is love, he becomes a lover—but must immediately begin to learn how to *express that love*. When a child is born, he is a human being, but embarks at once upon the process of learning to be the human he is.

So the newborn Christian is constantly faced with the choice of either living by the dictates of the Spirit of Christ and so die to self, or to assert self-will, which in the Scriptures is called *flesh*. The person in the light has seen too much to consistently choose the flesh, but it is still a real and often difficult choice. If he relapses into the flesh, he cannot live happily with himself.

The tension is always there, but to choose to live according to the true life within produces a lofty kind of life in the speech and actions:

> But the fruit of the Spirit is love, joy, peace, patience, kindness, goodness, faithfulness,
> gentleness, self-control; against such things there is no law.
> Now those who belong to Christ Jesus have crucified the flesh with its passions and desires.
>
> Galatians 5:22-23

Whenever Jesus spoke of the glorious benefits of the kingdom, He always spoke in the same breath about a death to self. Jesus said the road to life was through death to self-will. When describing the rest and ease of His life, He pointed out that it was only possible for those who came under His yoke and walked in obedience to Him. The one under the yoke of Christ finds it easy and the burden light:

> "Come to Me, all who are weary and heavy-laden, and I will give you rest.
> "Take My yoke upon you, and learn from Me, for I am gentle and humble in heart; and you shall find rest for your souls.
> "For my yoke is easy, and My load is light."
>
> Matthew 11:28-30

When a person chooses Christ's direction and rule and dies to self-rule, life comes together and the person is made whole. The *crisis* that brought a person to see that this One was the only life, was the beginning of the *process* of obedience and subsequent wholeness.

It's not that a person earns the right to the Father's presence and a place in His kingdom by acts of obedience. The place has been earned by Christ alone. But having been granted that acceptance by the grace of God, each Christian is called upon to bring his life into submission to what he sees as the only truth.

Isaiah saw this as the characteristic mark of the company on Zion—they wanted to submit their understanding of life to the law of God.

> And many peoples will come and say,
> "Come, let us go up to the mountain of
> the Lord,
> To the house of the God of Jacob;
> That He may teach us concerning His
> ways,
> And that we may walk in His paths."
> For the law will go forth from Zion,
> And the word of the Lord from Jeru-
> salem.
>
> Isaiah 2:3

In Ephesus were a company of all nations who had come to the true Zion in the Spirit and were candidates to be taught a new life in Jesus. Paul wrote and reminded them of who they *were* a foundation of what they would *become*:

> This I say, therefore, and testify in the
> Lord, that you should no longer walk as the

> rest of the Gentiles walk, in the futility of
> their mind,
> having their understanding darkened,
> being alienated from the life of God, because
> of the ignorance that is in them, because of
> the blindness of their heart;
> who, being past feeling, have given
> themselves over to licentiousness [lewdness],
> to work all uncleanness with greediness.
> But you have not so learned Christ,
> if indeed you have heard Him and have
> been taught by Him, as the truth is in Jesus:
> that you put off, concerning your former
> conduct, the old man which grows corrupt
> according to the deceitful lusts,
> and be renewed in the spirit of your
> mind,
> and that you put on the new man which
> was created according to God, in true
> righteousness and holiness.
>
> Ephesians 4:17-24, NKJV

In the light of who they were, they had to
change their habits and let the rule of Christ be
expressed: "Therefore be imitators of God, as
beloved children; and walk in love, just as Christ
also loved you, and gave Himself up for us . . ."
(Ephesians 5:1-2).

Paul went on to warn them that a profession of
Jesus as Lord that was not implemented in a life-
style that confessed Him as Lord, was an empty
form:

> For this you know, that no fornicator,
> unclean person, nor covetous man, who is an

> idolater, has any inheritance in the kingdom
> of Christ and God.
>
> Let no one deceive you with empty
> words, for because of these things the wrath
> of God comes upon the sons of disobedience.
>
> Therefore do not be partakers with them.
>
> For you were once darkness, but now
> you are light in the Lord. Walk as children
> of light.
>
> Ephesians 5:5-8, NKJV

People who live so differently as this are the laughingstock of the world. The world equates self-assertion with success. But here is a company that freely admits dependence and helplessness as their foundation for life. The world, in the insanity of independent self, mocks the sane ones as insane.

The Church is those who have died to this age, entered the kingdom of heaven, and yet continue to live here as visitors from another world. Jesus told them they were, "in the world, but not of it."

30

The *Different* Ones

The prophet Jeremiah had said that in the new covenant the Law would be written on the heart of man. The Law as expressed in the new covenant can be summed up in one word: *love*. "Owe nothing to anyone except to love one another; for he who loves his neighbor has fulfilled the law" (Romans 13:8).

Isaiah saw the same in a vision:

> And many peoples will come and say,
> "Come, let us go up to the mountain of the Lord,
> To the house of the God of Jacob;
> That He may teach us concerning His ways,
> And that we may walk in His paths."
> For the law will go forth from Zion,
> And the word of the Lord from Jerusalem.

> And He will judge between the nations,
> And will render decisions for many peoples;
> And they will hammer their swords into plowshares, and their spears into pruning hooks.
> Nation will not lift up sword against nation,
> And never again will they learn war.
>
> Isaiah 2:3-4

When men came to Mount Zion, they turned their weapons of destruction into tools for the benefit of their neighbors. The characteristic of the holy mountain was trust and open arms of love.

A sword is more than sharpened steel. The weapon of destruction is first forged in the spirit in thought processes and attitudes before it is fashioned into the form of a sword. The first action upon coming to the kingdom in Zion was to rid oneself of the weapons used to destroy others. That had to begin with a beating of thoughts and attitudes into love thoughts before swords were beaten into plowshares.

This was a risky business. In so doing, these people had yielded the right to be the aggressor, the destroyer with the sword. They had also become defenseless in an attack—they had surrendered the right to forge thoughts and attitudes of destruction. They could no longer fight back with words of murderous rage, let alone with weapons. They had come under the rule of the defenseless Lamb.

The Spirit has joined them to the Lamb. Jesus had emphasized that *by love among themselves* the world would know they were His disciples. The presence of this love is one of the tests for judging whether a man has passed from the kingdom of death and darkness into the kingdom of light and love. "We know that we have passed out of death into life, because we love the brethren. He who does not love abides in death" (I John 3:14).

Death is a sword in the heart, mouth, and—ultimately—in the hand. *Life* is to love neighbors, brothers, and even enemies. The kind of love found in Zion far exceeds all that man knows of love. The Law called men to love their neighbor as themselves, but Jesus said that the law of the kingdom of God was to love as He had loved them: "A new commandment I give to you, that you love one another, even as I have loved you, that you also love one another" (John 13:34).

The love of God within made this company a miracle community. Different races and tempera-ments flowing together and making up one new nation is a hopeless dream outside of the operation of the Spirit of Messiah. When the world comes into close quarters with each other, the very reverse of love comes into focus. Self pushes for the first place and grabs for all the honors it can get that will raise it above others. Anger, rage, loss of temper, jealousies and envies, resentment, and bitterness are normal in this atmosphere. But those translated out of that darkness by the resurrection of Messiah make up a new community of love with His love in them.

That inexhaustible river of love, however, has to be worked out into thought processes that have long been trained to think in terms of the lie. The love of God shed abroad has to be entrenched in attitudes and the

289

extremities of the life-style. The crisis that joins people to the Lamb must become the process whereby they become the lovers they have been made through that union.

The company of believers arrive on Mount Zion with swords in their hands. It is in the glory of Zion that they begin to actually do something about their weapons and change them into tools to benefit others. In receiving the free love of God revealed in Jesus, they are taken into a union with that love. They must now take deliberate action and exercise their free choice to harmonize with the rule and will of Him they have come to call Lord. Who, in the dimension of the Spirit of Christ, needs the sword of anger with which to destroy, or the spear of envy with which to fight for what another has? The reborn have seen that the love that dies for its enemies is the normal, and their swords must be brought into harmony with the Lord of true life.

In the world of darkness, man relates all other men to his own distorted self. They exist for his pleasure, to achieve his desires. On Mount Zion there is a new perspective, a new frame of reference—it is no longer *self* but the Lord Jesus Messiah. Every member of the kingdom is to be an expresser of Him and not of their own warped self.

This new love is the all-embracing life of the kingdom. It is the soil in which all the virtues of the Lord Jesus grow. Even as self-centeredness expresses itself in many negative ways, so love has many and varied positive expressions. Paul describes its various expressions in 1 Corinthians 13:4-6:

> Love is patient, love is kind, and is not
> jealous; love does not brag and is not
> arrogant,
>
> does not act unbecomingly; it does not
> seek its own, is not provoked, does not take
> into account a wrong suffered,
>
> does not rejoice in unrighteousness, but
> rejoices with the truth.

It is in these expressions that the inhabitants of Messiah's kingdom have to train themselves to love and bring their lives into harmony with Christ Jesus. So Paul often called upon the young communities to walk worthy of the Good News they were called to—to live out what God had worked in them.

The disciples in the upper room the night before He had died, had no relationship of love to each other. They were a group of isolated men who shared common adoration of Jesus and hoped to gain something when He became king.

After He breathed His Spirit into them, they gradually united in their attitudes, beliefs, and love for one another. This same miracle happened in all of the communities of Zion around the world, *but it did not happen automatically*. It was made manifest as the believers deliberately laid aside the old way of destroying one another and put on the new life in Christ. So Paul urged the believers in Colossae to do the same thing:

> Therefore consider the members of your
> earthly body as dead . . .
>
> now . . . put them all aside: anger, wrath,
> malice, slander, and abusive speech from
> your mouth.

> Do not lie to one another, since you laid aside the old self with its evil practices,
>
> and have put on the new self who is being renewed to a true knowledge according to the image of the One who created him, ...
>
> ... put on a heart of compassion, kindness, humility, gentleness and patience;
>
> bearing with one another, and forgiving each other, whoever has a complaint against any one; just as the Lord forgave you, so also should you.
>
> And beyond all these things put on love, which is the perfect bond of unity.
>
> Colossians 3:5, 8-10, 12-14

One of the first expressions of self that had to go was envy. The envious ultimately desire the removal of the object envied. Envy cannot bear the presence of the person who has more, whether in possessions, talents, or honors. It looks with displeasure and ill will at those more favored than itself. This is a natural feeling of the self that claws at its stolen throne. In seeing Jesus as Lord, man sees himself as he really is, a creature among fellow creatures who are *different—even from each other.*

He sees that not all have the same gifts. The strengths of one compliment the weaknesses in others. From that perspective, he sees that he is not to enter into envious competition with other Christians, but is to receive from them and minister to them. He learns to see that in areas of personal weakness, others are more important than he is:

> Do nothing from selfishness or empty
> conceit, but with humility of mind let each
> of you regard one another as more important
> than himself;
>
> do not merely look out for your own
> personal interests, but also for the interests
> of others.
>
> Philippians 2:3-4

The citizens of Zion are free to receive from each other in areas of weakness, and to give of their strengths. It is a community in covenant with each other, even as with the Lord Jesus.

When self-centered man is hurt, he finds it hard to forgive, for he has no basis for forgiveness. A sense of outraged justice within demands that *someone has to pay* for the wrong done. In his selfish frame of reference he has no other solution than to take it upon himself to pass judgment on the offender in rage and resentment. But members of the kingdom of Messiah have seen that in the final act of Jesus on the cross, someone has paid for all outraged justice. *They extend to their enemies a forgiveness already given through Jesus Christ.*

Because the nature of God's love is infinite, Jesus called the disciples to an unending forgiveness of those who hurt them: "Lord, how often shall my brother sin against me and I forgive him? Up to seven times?" Jesus said to him, "I do not say to you, up to seven times, but up to seventy times seven" (Matthew 18:21-22).

What Jesus was saying, of course, was that forgiveness is a way of life in His kingdom. On another

293

occasion when He spoke in a similar fashion, the response of the disciples was, "Increase our faith." They felt that an unusual amount of faith was needed for such a spiritual feat. Jesus refused to increase their faith: "If you had faith like a mustard seed, you would say to this mulberry tree, 'Be uprooted and be planted in the sea,' and it would obey you" (Luke 17:6).

He was telling them that in order to forgive they had to express with words what they already had. They could do this if they had a grain-of-mustard-seed understanding of the gospel—that His death paid for all sin. To speak words out of that faith and extend forgiveness to an enemy would tear up all the roots of bitterness and unlove.

God's love is different from human love, it does not operate on feelings that change, but on an unchanging will. That will was expressed among man in the final Word—Jesus Messiah. Now the members of His kingdom, whose wills are linked to His, express that forgiveness to the world around them with words.

To forgive as God has forgiven in Christ demands certain deliberate actions. Jesus illustrated the process of God's forgiveness in the story of the Prodigal Son. The boy has gone into a foreign country, disgraced the father's name, and squandered half a fortune. Now he returns and the father sees him while yet a great way from the farm and acts out his forgiveness: "But the father said to his slaves, 'Quickly bring out the best robe and put it on him, and put a ring on his hand and sandals on his feet; and bring the fattened calf, and kill it and let us eat and be merry; for this son of mine was dead, and has come to life again; he was lost, and has been found.' And they began to be merry" (Luke 15:22-24).

He was beating his sword into a plowshare, taking a series of deliberate actions to bring about the healing of his son's life. So the company on Zion are those who take their mind and their attitudes and reshape them in the light of the cross.

Such action is against all natural feelings. To choose to obey the Spirit of love within was a death to self-will that operated out of feelings. The kingdom of darkness was to live under the authority of emotion and feeling reaction. The kingdom of the new-born was under the command of Jesus the Lord, and born of choices made in the light of love.

The world despised them. These pockets of love blazed into the darkness showing up the distortion of self-centeredness. They wrote sneeringly of these Christians who loved one another and then went on to kill them. The church responded as their king, "Lord, lay not this sin at their charge."

31

Kingdom Living Here and Now

Joy is the registered emotion of the man who has God for his center and frame of reference. Joy is a constant, unmoved by the changing course of events, for it is rooted in the unchanging God. It rests in God's perfect purposes of holy love, goodness, wisdom, and Almighty power that bring His plans to pass. Even the darkness is made to serve the triumphant end of God. The Lord joys in His own perfection, because He is unable as the perfect One to rejoice in anything less than the perfect. Man was created to share the joy God has in Himself, and be unmoved by the swirling currents of events around him.

But man switched centers. He plunged into the darkness built on the lie that he is the center of the universe and the framework into which all must be fitted. In that moment, he created a monster called *happiness*. Happiness is the distorted self's substitute for joy. It depends on the nature of the *happenings* around man, whether they please him or fit his framework. If they do, then he is *happy*. If they cut across the framework of self, then he helplessly wishes that they would *unhappen,* and so describes himself as *unhappy*. Life becomes a journey through a desert following the mirage of happiness—a fantasy where all people, events, and even God are doing what the individual man wishes them to do. Happiness is the ultimate of the distorted ego, the harmonizing of all to the self-willing self.

Such a fantasy does not happen. It is part of the insanity of the darkness. Pursuing happiness, man spends most of his time in unhappiness—and when he finds happiness for a fleeting moment, it mysteriously evaporates, and the search begins again.

In this futile pursuit man will change jobs, neighborhoods, countries, spouse, and even his religion. But all that he finds is a passing emotion described as "the passing pleasures of sin" (Hebrews 11:25). The Book of Proverbs describes this kind of happiness as the burning of kindling sticks. It blazes and then is left as a heap of ashes. So man lives in the ashes of the brief moments of happiness. He is bored, complaining, and un-thankful.

This attitude toward life in the darkness trains people in unthankfulness. Every detail of life that does not fit into the framework of self is the subject of complaint. In fact, complaint becomes the basic language of the lie. With some it has become their only language and way of life. They pass all moments of their lives through the grid of their distorted selves, and express the resulting frustrations in tirades of complaint. The inhabitants of the darkness are withered humans and mere ghosts of what they were created to be.

Although conversation is addressed to other humans, it is ultimately addressed to God. The complaining between man and man is actually directed at God: "Your grumblings are . . . against the Lord" (Exodus 16:8). To complain is to suggest that God's love—and His wisdom and power to achieve His love-purpose—is highly suspect. It implies that God is lying to us when He speaks of His care for us.

Joy, the constant rest and rejoicing in who God is and what He is accomplishing, is found in the act of worship. Only as man is in right relationship to God can he know joy. The psalmists saw joy as a result of living in dependence upon God: "In Thy presence is fulness of joy; in Thy right hand there are pleasures forever" (Psalms 16:11).

To the believing Israelite, religion was not a dismal affair; it was rejoicing in God with heart, mind, and body. They were even commanded to rejoice in their coming together for religious feasts. The psalmists called upon the worshipers to involve the whole person, spirit, soul, and body in the celebration of God. The Hebrews saw all creation moving in joyous praise to the Creator. The hills danced and sang, the trees clapped their hands, and the whole earth and sky shouted in ecstasy at the sight of God's glory.

Man shared in the joy that God had in Himself. The Lord is never frustrated, complaining, or in despair. With unbeginning infinity of joy, He rejoices in the perfection of His unchanging self. The final uncovering of that perfect holiness was in the act of Jesus Messiah and is the focal point of His joy.

He bequeathed His joy to the disciples: "These things I have spoken to you, that My joy may be in you, and that your joy may be made full" (John 15:11). Later the same night He reassured them, "Therefore you, too, now have sorrow—but I will see you again, and your heart will rejoice, and no one takes your joy away from you" (John 16:22). This was a joy not known in the darkness. It was a new kind of joy centered, not in self, but in God and His glory. This joy could never become *unjoy,* for it was more real than all the sorrows that could assault it. Its object, and therefore its source, was the unchanging God.

The prophets saw it as an everlasting joy with which the inhabitants of Zion wore halos (Isaiah 51:11). "Everlasting" is defined as without beginning or ending—so it was a joy caused by nothing in time and therefore not to be uncaused by anything in time.

Jesus spoke of this joy beginning when man came out of the darkness of death into the kingdom of heaven (see Luke 15:5-6, 32). The sinner who believes in Jesus for eternal life, finds himself engulfed in that joy. At that moment he rarely knows why he is rejoicing, and is only aware of being at one with God and filled with holy joy.

When the Spirit came into the disciples on the night of resurrection, the joy began and caused them to be daily in the temple praising God: "And they returned to Jerusalem with great joy, and were continually in the temple, praising God" (Luke 24:52-53). On the day of Pentecost when the Spirit enveloped them, they were men and women in an ecstasy of being in two worlds at once—the world of the natural and the world of the Spirit. Their lips overflowed as they spoke of the wonderful works of God in a language adequate for their overflowing spirits. So great was their joy that bystanders mocked, "They are full of sweet wine" (Acts 2:13). The joy and rejoicing of heaven had come among men.

> The Spirit of the Lord God is upon me,
> Because the Lord has anointed me
> To bring good news to the afflicted;
> He has sent me to bind up the broken-
> hearted,
> To proclaim liberty to captives,
> And freedom to prisoners;
> To proclaim the favorable year of the
> Lord,
> And the day of vengeance of our God;
> To comfort all who mourn,
> To grant those who mourn in Zion,
> Giving them a garland instead of ashes,
> The oil of gladness instead of mourning,
> The mantle of praise instead of a spirit
> of fainting.
>
> Isaiah 61:1-3

The men of darkness could not comprehend anyone's being in a state of ecstasy through worshiping God. To man in his sin, God was a source of fear—not joy. In the beginning Adam fled to hide from God, and ever since then, man looked upon the holy One with dread. To many on the day of Pentecost, the joy of those in the new kingdom of the Spirit could only have been caused by the effects of alcohol. Such hilarity could only be achieved by being desensitized to life as it really was. They did not know it, but they were seeing people who suddenly not only saw things as they were, but saw, from God's view, the whole truth. Their senses were not drugged, but rather made so alive by the Spirit that they were acutely aware of the invisible half of the universe and could not help but rejoice with joy unspeakable at what was now known to them.

As the Church thrust its way through paganism, the most arresting mark—next to their love for one another—was joy. At times when they suffered persecution and loss of all things, love and joy radiated through their lives. Jesus had spoken of this phenomenon: "Blessed are you when men revile you, and persecute you, and say all kinds of evil against you falsely, on account of Me" (Matthew 5:11).

When the authorities confiscated their property in their hatred for members of Messiah's kingdom, they did not retaliate or complain, but rather rejoiced: "For you . . . accepted joyfully the seizure of your property, knowing that you have for yourselves a better possession and an abiding one" (Hebrews 10:34). They had found a new center of joy; not in things owned, but in the Lord *Himself*. It was the same joy in God that Habakkuk had expressed:

> Though the fig tree should not blossom,
> And there be no fruit on the vines,
> Though the yield of the olive should fail,
> And the fields produce no food,
> Though the flock should be cut off from
> the fold,
>> and there be no cattle in the stalls,
>> Yet I will exult in the Lord,
>> I will rejoice in the God of my salvation.
>>> Habakkuk 3:17-18

A life-style and language of joy does not happen automatically. To come to Zion is to learn a new language. It is to set the will in resolve to praise God, the center of all things, regardless of what feelings may say. The determination of David becomes the expression of the member of Messiah's kingdom:

> I will bless the Lord at all times;
> His praise shall continually be in my
> mouth.
> My soul shall make its boast in the Lord;
> The humble shall hear it and rejoice.
> O magnify the Lord with me,
> And let us exalt His name together.
>> Psalms 34:1-3

The new way of life was a new way of talking that was impregnated with thanksgiving and joyous expression to God: "Speaking to one another in psalms and hymns and spiritual songs, singing and making melody with your heart to the Lord; always giving thanks for all things in the name of our Lord Jesus Christ to God, even the Father" (Ephesians 5:19-20). Instead of filtering life through the distorted self, the earlier believers saw all in reference to Jesus the Lord and gave thanks.

The life Himself surged out of the tomb, entered into the dead spirits of men and women and raised them into the dimension of the Spirit. Alive in their God, they knew the joy for which they had been created. It was a joy that could not be hidden—it showed up in their attitudes, conversation, life-style, and found best expression in their worship in the Spirit.

In any company of Messiah's kingdom, the vision of the prophet is seen in its new covenant fulfillment:

> Then the eyes of the blind will be opened,
> And the ears of the deaf will be unstopped.
> Then the lame will leap like a deer,
> And the tongue of the dumb will shout with joy.
> . . . But the redeemed will walk there,
> And the ransomed of the Lord will return,
> And come with joyful shouting to Zion,
> With everlasting joy upon their heads.
> They will find gladness and joy,
> And sorrow and sighing will flee away.
> Isaiah 35:5-6, 9-10

The day of Messiah has come! Kingdom living is here and now!

Epilogue

Nearly two thousand years have passed since the empty tomb and the coronation of the King. Since then, there has always been a company on earth who have lived in the Spirit, the kingdom of Messiah on earth. In these last hundred years, tens of thousands have entered the kingdom by the new birth and have entered the dimension of being filled with the Spirit. The Church today is awakening to an awareness that "the kingdom of God is . . . righteousness and peace and joy in the Holy Spirit (Romans 14:17).

The Lordship of Jesus is as real today as when He first sat upon His throne to rule in the midst of His enemies. The Holy Spirit, through the Scriptures, brings His commands to us. We are making costly choices to love one another, forgive as we have been forgiven, and bring our whole life-style to glorify God through His Christ.

What of the future? The hope of the Church is the consummation of the kingdom when the last enemy—death—shall be destroyed. It is already conquered in Christ, but we await His return and the resurrection of the body.

> But we do not want you to be un-
> informed, brethren, about those who are
> asleep, that you may not grieve, as do the rest
> who have no hope.
>
> For if we believe that Jesus died and rose
> again, even so God will bring with Him those
> who have fallen asleep in Jesus.
>
> For this we say to you by the word of the
> Lord, that we who are alive, and remain until
> the coming of the Lord, shall not precede
> those who have fallen asleep.
>
> For the Lord Himself will descend from
> heaven with a shout, with the voice of the
> archangel, and with the trumpet of God; and
> the dead in Christ shall rise first.
>
> Then we who are alive and remain shall
> be caught up together with them in the
> clouds to meet the Lord in the air, and thus
> we shall always be with the Lord.
>
> Thessalonians 4:13-17

Of us it is said, "For our citizenship is in heaven, from which also we eagerly wait for a Savior, the Lord Jesus Christ; who will transform the body of our humble state into conformity with the body of His glory, by the exertion of the power that He has even to subject all things to Himself" (Philippians 3:20-21).

In a world that centers on self and builds its Babels, the Christian knows that all will one day be swept away to bring in the ultimate of the ancient promises. It will be the promised time when the whole world will be under the rule of Messiah.

> But the day of the Lord will come like a
> thief, in which the heavens will pass away

with a roar and the elements will be destroyed with intense heat, and the earth and its works will be burned up.

Since all these things are to be destroyed in this way, what sort of people ought you to be in holy conduct and godliness,

looking for and hastening the coming of the day of God, on account of which the heavens will be destroyed by burning, and the elements will melt with intense heat!

But according to His promise we are looking for new heavens and a new earth, in which righteousness dwells.

2 Peter 3:10-13

They will not hurt or destroy in all My holy mountain,

For the earth will be full of the knowledge of the Lord

As the waters cover the sea.

Isaiah 11:9

The last words of our Lord Jesus Messiah to His Church were, "I am coming quickly." To which the Church responds, "Amen. Come, Lord Jesus."